ALCHEMYZE IT!

Alchemyze It!

"In all my years of Vistage coaching, it was challenging to describe the power of a great marketing message to my members. Eric saves the day with his new book, Alchemyze It!. *In just six simple steps he shows entrepreneurs how to take their average story about their company to a truly remarkable one! I suggest his book as prescribed reading for Vistage members who are committed to scaling their business"*

FRANK DAY, VISTAGE CHAIR
WINNER OF THE DON COPE MEMORIAL AWARD

"I've had the privilege of leading marketing teams for some of the world's most recognized brands as well as fast-growing technology startups. Often, the greatest impediment to achieving revenue growth is aligning the executive team behind a customer-centric messaging strategy. This is essential for a business to achieve its goals. In Alchemyze It!, *Eric provides a fantastic framework for developing messaging that will break through the clutter and accelerate growth. The book is full of anecdotes that bring the framework to life. It is hard to imagine a reader not going back to their company with innovative ideas for how to differentiate their brand in the market."*

MITCH ROSE
SVP MARKETING, BILLTRUST

"To win in business today, you need to stand out. You need a marketing message that differentiates you from the competition and grabs the attention of your target audience. Alchemyze It! *provides a simple six-step process that will help you create a message that does just that. If you want to achieve real differentiation, connect with your target audience, and get stronger results, this is the guide you've been waiting for. Thanks, Eric!"*

AMY HOLTZ
CERTIFIED EOS IMPLEMENTER®

"*Alchemize It! offers entrepreneurs a compelling step-by-step process, brought to life with real stories, of how you can claim the hidden power that will transform your business from the ordinary to extraordinary. Reading this book will give you confidence and an easy-to-follow roadmap to step into the power (you already have).*"

BARRY KAPLAN
FOUNDER OF SHIFT 180

"*Having had the privilege of working directly with Eric, I can confidently say that* Alchemyze It! *is a game-changer, helping us not just survive but thrive by uncovering our unique value and communicating it effectively to the medical market. His ability to turn the ordinary into the extraordinary is truly remarkable, and this book is a testament to his genius in the art of differentiation.*"

JOE CARBERRY
CEO, LYMPHA PRESS

"Alchemyze It! *is a must for companies running on EOS. It addresses a few simple things you can do without spending big money to take your company to the next level. It will take your marketing strategy to the next level. Well done!*"

ROSS GIBBS
EXPERT EOS IMPLEMENTER®

"*I've been struggling to pinpoint what truly sets my company apart. After reading* Alchemyze It!, *I finally had the clarity I needed. The strategies outlined in this book helped me identify the unique qualities that make us remarkable. By focusing on these strengths, we've seen a significant increase in revenue and customer satisfaction. I highly recommend this book to any business owner looking to elevate their brand and drive growth.*"

TOM BEMILLER, PRESIDENT
AUREUS AUTO BODY

"Alchemyze It! *was exactly what I needed to tell my company's story in a way that actually captures attention. I've struggled with the storytelling part— how to really communicate what makes us unique. This book broke it down so well! The process was simple to follow, and now my company story feels fresh and remarkable. If you're a business owner who knows your company is great but can't quite put it into words, Eric's book is your answer."*

BARRETT ERSEK, CEO
HOLGANIX

"In addition to being a workbook for all frustrated small business owners who want to grow their business and aren't sure how to attract prospective buyers, Alchemyze It! will be an invaluable resource for professional EOS Implementers* and self-implementers of EOS when working on the marketing section of the EOS Vision/Traction Organizer."

ED CALLAHAN
EMERITUS EOS IMPLEMENTER*

"Are you an entrepreneurial company tired of your message being lost in the noise? Then Alchemyze It! is the help you need. Eric guides you through a step-by-step journey using storytelling to breathe life into your everyday experiences, turning them into powerful differentiators that will help your brand stand out in the crowd and captivate your audiences. A must-read!"

RICHARD PRICE
ENTREPRENEUR, CERTIFIED EOS IMPLEMENTER® AND COACH

EOS
—— IMPACT ——

Published by Igniting Souls
PO Box 43, Powell, OH 43065
IgnitingSouls.com

ISBN: 978-1-63680-494-1 (paperback)
        978-1-63680-495-8 (hardback)
        978-1-63680-496-5(epub)

Available in paperback, hardcover, e-book, and audiobook.

All Scripture quotations, unless otherwise indicated, are taken from the Holy Bible, New International Version®, NIV®. Copyright © 1973, 1978, 1984, 2011 by Biblica, Inc.™ Used by permission of Zondervan. All rights reserved worldwide. www.zondervan. com The "NIV" and "New International Version" are trademarks registered in the United States Patent and Trademark Office by Biblica, Inc.™

Any Internet addresses (websites, blogs, etc.) and telephone numbers printed in this book are offered as a resource. They are not intended in any way to be or imply an endorsement by Igniting Souls, nor does Igniting Souls vouch for the content of these sites and numbers for the life of this book.

Some names and identifying details may have been changed to protect the privacy of individuals.

The superscript symbol IP listed throughout this book is known as the unique certification mark created and owned by Instant IP™. Its use signifies that the corresponding expression (words, phrases, chart, graph, etc.) has been protected by Instant IP™ via smart contract. Instant IP™ is designed with the patented smart contract solution (US Patent: 11,928,748), which creates an immutable time-stamped first layer and fast layer identifying the moment in time an idea is filed on the blockchain. This solution can be used in defending intellectual property protection. Infringing upon the respective intellectual property, i.e., IP, is subject to and punishable in a court of law.

Published in 2025
Written by Eric Keiles with Derek Lewis
AlchemyzeIt.com

Publishing and design services: MelindaMartin.me
Editor: Derek Lewis

ALCHEMYZE IT!

A Proven Process
To Differentiate and Scale
Your Entrepreneurial Business

Eric Keiles

with Derek Lewis

For Bonnie,
who always supported my entrepreneurial journey
(even after I "retired")

For the thousands of entrepreneurs
who took the leap of faith to follow my advice

Contents

FOREWORD

If you don't have anything remarkable to say about your business, don't spend any money on marketing.

There are better ways to burn your cash.

At this point in my life, I estimate that I've worked with roughly a thousand entrepreneurs and business leaders over nearly forty years, from running marketing for a Xerox division to creating a growth strategy for a single self-employed consultant. In all that time, one thing has become crystal clear to me.

Nobody knows what they're doing.

Not with marketing, anyway.

That's a slight exaggeration. I have worked with some entrepreneurs who were on the right path and needed a little push to expand their vision of what was possible. But the vast majority of companies don't know how to effectively market their business to get enough leads to land enough sales to grow like they've dreamed. The more owners and leaders I work with, the more I realize how prevalent this problem is. It's a pandemic in business.

Add to that new regulations, privacy concerns, social media, and now even artificial intelligence and it's no wonder people are overwhelmed. Things are more confusing than ever.

Faced with this, most CEOs and business owners simply end up throwing money at the problem, hoping it will fix itself. Google Ads? Facebook ads? TikToks? AI chatbots? Digital billboards?

Direct mail? Email campaigns? They buy them all and hope something sticks!

Einstein once said, "Insanity is doing the same thing over and over again and expecting different results." Today's approach to marketing is insane. If you switch from newspaper ads to online ads, it might look like you're doing something different. You're not. You're still throwing money at a problem you don't understand. You may waste your budget differently this quarter than you did last, but fundamentally you're doing the same thing. Over and over again. Hope is not a strategy.

Say it with me: *Hope is not a strategy.*

Sure, you "hope" your rainmaker closes a big account. You "hope" marketing turns up a treasure trove of qualified leads. You "hope" you'll buy the winning lottery ticket. Hope all you want. But don't depend on it to make payroll.

That's why I love Eric's book. It's not about using the latest gimmick, some new tech, or chasing the fad of the month. It's about a serious, down-to-earth, timeless, universal, practical, proven, and effective strategy to share your business with the world.

Over twenty years ago, Eric and I founded our marketing agency with the unique purpose of differentiating companies from their competition. I am gratified to see that, even in "retirement," Eric still has the same passion he did when we started. He's taken everything we learned together along with his unique insights to create the Alchemyze process as the much-needed complement to EOS. I think the name is perfect. Turning seemingly ordinary companies into something remarkably extraordinary? That's what Eric's done his entire professional life, not just with clients but with our businesses as well as his own. He has a gift for creating marketing messaging or even more accurately...entrepreneurial storytelling.

No matter the size of your company or your marketing budget and regardless of your industry or market, if you'll follow Eric's process, you will wind up where you want to be: at the helm of a business your customers rave about, your competition gawks at, and your prospects never stop hearing about.

It will be, in a word, "remarkable."

Mike Lieberman
co-author of *Smash the Funnel*,
Fire Your Sales Team Today,
and *Reality Marketing Revolution*

READ THIS FIRST

I didn't write this book for people in the marketing department. It's for the founders, owners, and CEOs in a position to overhaul how your company does business. It's about creating a strategy that changes its identity. If that scares you, then **don't waste your time** reading this.

The Alchemyze process isn't about marketing. At least, not the way you think about it. Alchemyze is about creating a differentiation strategy that sets you apart from everyone else.

If you're ready to do something—and create something—extraordinary, then go download the companion workbook before you start reading:

www.AlchemyzeIt.com

I created the Alchemyze process specifically for companies running on EOS, but if you don't know what that is, don't worry. It works on its own, too. Throughout the book, you'll see side notes where I "translate" EOS-speak into plain English so you won't ever feel lost.

Now, let's get remarkable.

1

From Lead to Gold (to Green!)

"In its simplest form, alchemy is the process of taking something ordinary and turning it into something extraordinary—sometimes in a way that cannot be explained. Alchemy is seen in the way an artist can, quite magically, transform a heap of scrap metal into a breathtaking piece of art. I believe that in the business world, we are all trying to create alchemy. We want to take something ordinary and turn it into the extraordinary."

—YASMIN BELO-OSAGIE, FOUNDER OF SHE LEADS AFRICA

R emember the fairy tale *Rumpelstiltskin*?

You might recall the story centered around an evil little man who could spin straw into gold. This is a literal fairytale, but once upon a time, people took this idea seriously. For a few thousand years, humankind believed that with the right magic and science, we could turn something ordinary—like straw or lead—into something extraordinary, like gold. In medieval Europe, they called this "alchemy."

I've worked with hundreds of companies and taught thousands of entrepreneurs how to take the story about their ordinary business and, with a little bit of magic, turn it into something remarkable. Often, they have everything they need. Most of my work simply takes what they already do and helps them tell a better story. Some require a slight shift to their operations to position themselves as "remarkable," but for the most part, they have everything they need to differentiate themselves. They simply are bad at storytelling.

That's why I call the process "Alchemyze."

Not Sexy but Safe

Let me tell you about a pretty unsexy company that dramatically changed its story. They are a distributor of safety products, selling mostly to companies that have factories, warehouses, and distribution centers. They sell steel-toed boots, safety glasses, gloves, and hard hats. You get the picture. When the founder started the company back in the 1940s, his focus was, "How much stuff can I sell?"

Nothing wrong with that. I'm an entrepreneur myself who's founded, owned, operated, and sold quite a few businesses. Selling your stuff is the lifeblood of any business. But back in the 40s, the founder didn't have the competition we have today. These days, Amazon carries virtually everything this company does.

The first question I ask in my seminars is, "Why are you the obvious choice to do business with? On your note card, write down three reasons someone should choose to do business with you over your competitors." It's a trick. I already know what they're going to write because everybody always writes some variation of the exact same things:

1. We offer good quality at a good price.

2. We have good people.

3. We have X years of experience.

Everyone says that. And it doesn't matter whether or not it's true. Your customers hear the exact same thing from every one of your competitors. You need to give them a reason to choose you instead of someone else. Forget about edging someone out. You need more than an edge. You need to be the *obvious* choice. As in, *there is no question in your customer's mind that you're the best one for the job.*

When the founder of the safety products company retired and passed the reins to his daughter, that was her challenge. She competed with other companies selling some of the same products to the same customers.

How could she get across that her company was different?

As I said, there's nothing really sexy about work boots and hard hats. All safety equipment is really "just in case" products. Just in case somebody drops a hammer from the third story. Just in case a boxcutter slips. Just in case the belt breaks while the engine's running. Nobody wants to think about these worst-case scenarios. Nobody wants to think about them or their coworkers getting hurt.

So how do you market something nobody wants to think about?

In a consultation with the current CEO, I asked, "Okay, answer this: What's the big story here? What are you really trying to do? What makes you get out of bed every morning?"

She said, "You know . . . if we could get all the employees of our clients—all those folks that work in the factories, warehouses, and distribution centers we sell to—if we can get every one of them home safely each night, we would have fulfilled our mission."

Bingo!

"Everybody goes home safe tonight."

That became not just the company slogan but its *core purpose.* Five words captured the beating heart of its people. It became a rallying cry for everyone inside and outside the company. The company switched from selling gloves and glasses to getting workers home safely at the end of every day.

Today, when you go to their competitors' websites, they talk about having the lowest prices, the best customer service, and the fastest shipping. When you go to their website, you can feel that they care about the safety of your employees. They're more than a safety products distributor. They're your trusted partner in taking care of your people. If you're in charge of safety at your warehouse, who would you rather do business with? Someone trying to sell you stuff? Or someone who wants to keep your people safe? Now, they are clearly the superior option.

The obvious choice.

We Alchemyzed their company, turning their ordinary story into something remarkable. They didn't need to spend $50,000 for a new state-of-the-art website. No Google ads. They didn't need to rent digital billboards for $10,000 a month each. Sure, over time, they redid their marketing to reflect their new mission, but they had those dollars budgeted anyway. My point is that differentiating your company is about working smarter, not harder.

Forget Marketing. Think Differentiation.

Speaking of spending the same amount of money . . .

I want to show you how powerful a little difference can be. Let's say a gizmo manufacturer sells each gizmo for $50,000. Let's pretend they get 10 sales leads a month. To keep things simple, let's say their closing rate—how many customers they land out of every 10 leads they have—is 10%, which is about average for their industry.

So, they get 10 leads a month. They close 1 prospect. They generate $50,000 in revenue.

That comes out to $600,000 in annual revenue.

Cool.

Then they come across a copy of *Alchemyze It!* They're tired of fighting over the same scraps as everyone else. Their company has hit a plateau. They figure it can't hurt, so they give it the old college try. They walk through the six-step process to find a way to communicate how their company is different than the other guys. Even with an imperfect understanding of how to Alchemyze their business, they still get a lot of it right. They "find their lane" and focus on it like a laser beam. Their salespeople begin talking about the unique way their company does business—things their prospects don't hear from the competition. After all that, they only close one more customer per month.

Just one? That sounds discouraging. Until you do the math.

One extra customer a month doubles their close rate from 10% to 20%. Instead of $50,000 a month, they gross $100,000. Annual sales jump from $600,000 to a whopping $1.2 million . . . all without spending one extra penny. They simply found a better way to talk about their company and stand out from the crowd.

What would the impact of a few extra customers a month do for your top line? Could you even double your average close rate? If you're anything like the companies I've worked with, from screw manufacturers to wealth managers to tech startups, that's an easy yes. Plenty of my clients have gone from 2% to 4%, from 5% to 10%, and even from 15% to 30%.

Again . . . *without spending any extra money.*

That's the power of an effective differentiation strategy.

Companies spend a fortune on advertising (a specific tactic) without formulating a real strategy, such as who they're uniquely positioned to work with and how to create a compelling way to communicate with them. Without a way to tell your potential customers how you're different, your company looks like every other one out there.

An acquaintance of mine heads a billion-dollar company's engineering team. He told me the story of the time a newly promoted maintenance supervisor at one of their manufacturing plants approached him with a problem. He needed to replace the plant's industrial air compressor.

"Sam, you know I've got to pick a vendor for this? Well, it's come down to these two. Their bids are both right at $60,000. They have the same warranties, about the same shipping times, and roughly the same reputations. I've got to choose one, but I can't tell how one is better than the other. What would you do?"

After spending a couple of minutes going through the details, the engineer came to the same conclusion as the maintenance supervisor. There really wasn't a difference between the two bids. So, Sam gave him some advice based on his years in engineering and spearheading retrofits and greenfield construction sites on four continents.

"Just flip a coin."

You'd be kidding yourself if you think your customers don't sometimes do the same thing. They may not reach in their pocket for a literal coin, but far too often they do a mental coin toss. They decide to go with you because they like your logo better. They chose the competition because the receptionist was nice to them. They use all sorts of meaningless measures to help them decide who to pick. This happens because *they cannot see a difference between you and everybody else.* None of you are remarkable.

Webster defines remarkable as "worthy of being, or likely to be, noticed, especially as being uncommon or extraordinary." You want to stand out. You want to be uncommon. You don't want to be ordinary but extra-ordinary.

If you've been in business for more than three years, you are definitely doing something remarkable. Otherwise, your company would have fallen by the wayside like most do. You sell, do, or provide something unique your particular customers appreciate.

With the businesses I've worked with, I find they often have an extraordinary approach to business. The problem is the outside perception does not reflect their inside reality. To be blunt, they suck at storytelling. They don't know how to translate what they do into a marketing message that resonates with the people they love to work with. When we align how they operate with how their prospects perceive them, sales and marketing take off!

How?

With alchemy.

Alchemyze Your Company in 6 Easy Steps

While this book stands on its own merit and works for any company, I wrote it with companies running on EOS in mind. If you don't know what that is, don't worry. I'll explain the basics in chapter two and put boxes like this throughout the book to "translate" EOS-speak into plain English. The beauty of Alchemyze is that it works even if you don't use EOS. But if you want to add rocket fuel to your business, you absolutely should check out EOS, the Entrepreneurial Operating System.

As a practitioner of the Entrepreneurial Operating System (EOS) as well as an EOS Implementer®, I preach process, process, process. If you want to scale your business, you have to turn everything you can into a repeatable process. As you might have already guessed, Alchemyze is no different. The steps are to answer these six questions:

1. What's your vision? (your "Big Hairy Audacious Goal" or BHAG)

2. Who's your perfect client? (persona)

3. What's that nagging fear at the back of their mind? (core problems)

4. How can we provide those solutions in a remarkable way? (Alchemyze it!)

5. How can we best communicate that? (the "big story")

6. How can we say that in a direct and emotionally compelling way? (headlines)

Don't forget to go download your free companion workbook to help you Alchemyze your business at www.AlchemyzeIt.com

We'll go into a little more detail about each of those steps in the next chapter (and throughout the rest of the book), but the important thing here is that Alchemyze is a step-by-step process. Most business owners want to jump to step six and come up with an attention-grabbing headline for an online ad or an impressive-sounding tagline. Most skip the third step altogether. Instead of asking what their customers really want, they just try to find a way to sell as much as they can to as many people as they can. With that approach, they never even stop to ask the first question: "Are we selling to the right people in the first place?"

Using this approach, I have Alchemyzed digital marketing agencies, commercial construction companies, banks and credit unions, industrial paint manufacturers, landscaping contractors, accounting firms, fastener fabricators, and funeral homes. Like EOS itself, Alchemyze is a business process that works regardless of your business, industry, or market.

Let me walk you through a full story of Alchemyzing a company.

I once worked with Kate, the owner of a wonderful construction company out of Los Angeles. They did great work and had great testimonials. Then again, so did all of their competitors. Or, at least, that's what it looked like to potential clients on the outside looking at all their options.

The firm could do just about any type of commercial construction. And that was the problem. Kind of hard to be the obvious choice when you sell everything to everybody. I kicked off the Alchemyze process by asking Kate who she loved working with. What were her favorite types of projects? Could she describe her perfect client?

Although her company had made a lot of money constructing brand-new buildings from the ground up, she preferred office build-outs. Say you have a growing law firm. Five years ago, you leased an office space of 10,000 square feet, but you've since outgrown it. With your lease soon expiring, you want to move to a space twice that size. And you want to do it right. You don't just want 20,000 square feet. You want 20,000 square feet designed expressly for how your law firm works.

Kate loved these types of projects and had developed something of a specialty in them. So, the first question was, "Who is your perfect client?" In her case, it was office managers. They're traditionally the ones in charge of office moves and build-outs. The law partners (or whoever was running the company) didn't want to be involved in the nitty-gritty details of designing an office space and picking out cubicle colors. They leave all of that up to their office manager or firm administrator.

The next step in the process was easy. What are the core problems Kate's construction firm could solve for an office manager doing a buildout? Clients always worry about finishing on time and on budget. More importantly, once the law firm moves, they want the attorneys to be happy.

One of the major sore spots for these types of office moves is called a "punch list." Basically, it's the mop-up stuff. After moving in, someone discovers an electrical outlet that doesn't have power. One of the partners' office doors doesn't close properly. The toilet in the handicapped bathroom runs continuously. The dishwasher in the breakroom wasn't screwed into the counter and pulls away from the wall when it's opened.

Since the buildout is already finished, the construction company has moved on to the next project. They will send someone out to fix all these little things (either because of the contract or because of good customer service) . . . but when? The office manager often has to hound their contractor to come back out. Even then, the mop-up person doesn't always fix everything on the list.

Kate hated the punch list, in part because customers gave her so much grief about it. But she also hated leaving customers with a bad taste in their mouth. So, she would send one of her construction people 30 days before the end of the project to start identifying punch list items ahead of time. Their responsibility was to cure all of the issues on the punch list before the project concluded. When it came time to hand over the keys to the client, there was no punch list.

I said, "Kate, that's amazing. I'm sure every office manager wants that. What do you call that?"

She frowned. "I . . . I don't call it anything. It's just something we do."

She had never thought about naming it. That's typical. Kate was amazing at project management, but she wasn't a storyteller. It never occurred to her that doing something different like that could be a differentiator.

We decided to call it the *Zero Punch List Countdown*. The next time she pitched her firm to a potential client, she walked them through the typical construction process. But at the end of the process, she revealed the Zero Punch List Countdown. Thirty days before the end of the project, Kate would assign a Punch List Manager. This person would show up to the construction site wearing a white lab coat embroidered with "Punch List Manager" and walk through the entire office with the client. Together, they would identify all the little to-do items left. The manager would go back to the office, type up the list, and send an email to the office manager.

Five days later, they would send the office manager another email. One section of the email would show what punch list items had been fixed, which ones were left over, and what new ones had been identified since the previous email.

Five days after that—at this point, twenty days before the end of the project—they would send another update email. Then again fifteen days out. Then ten. Then five, four, three, two, and one. The countdown to zero items on the punch list.

Not only did Kate land that prospect but her sales close rate on new projects went through the roof. People loved the idea of working with a construction company that cared about the small details so many construction people might overlook. They loved the idea of not having to hound the firm to come back and fix something that should have been done right in the first place.

How much did it cost Kate to create the Zero Punch List Countdown? Simply the price of a white lab coat with "Punch List Manager" embroidered on it. And once the manager started showing up at the promised thirty days before close, the office managers started talking to other people about this construction company "who sends out a guy in a lab coat to make sure everything is perfect *before* the move-in!" It generated so much buzz that Kate's referrals began to grow incredibly fast. For the cost of a lab coat and a small change in behavior, Kate started getting better quality leads on the project types she loved doing anyway.

If you're counting, that was steps one through four of Alchemyze.

From there, we crafted a compelling story about the construction firm wanting to make office build-outs headache-free. That's step five. The last one, step six, seemed pretty obvious. When they updated their website and marketing materials, the headline was simply, "Love Your New Office From Day One."

Alchemyze can be more complicated than Kate's example, and we'll go into some in-depth case studies with a few other companies, but you get the gist. Starting with step one naturally led to step two and so on. Following the process leads to turning something ordinary into something remarkable.

In EOS, the "3 Uniques" are simply three things that make your company stand out from the competition. They serve as the answer to why prospects should do business with your firm.

EOS says your company needs to have "3 Uniques." After working with Kate to identify a few more problems the office managers had and creating some remarkable solutions (that tied into the theme of loving their office), her construction firm became the *obvious choice to do business with.*

Don't you want the same for your business?

In the Alchemyze workbook, do "Step #1: Differentiation."

2

What the Heck Is EOS®?

"I used to worry about 100 different things. Once I learned there were six components to my business and I focused only on those, those 100 different things I'd been worrying about went away. EOS made running the business simpler."

—GINO WICKMAN IN *TRACTION*

J ust before COVID, I was at my brother-in-law's suburban home. It was a beautiful sunny day. Just right for a refreshing dip in his pool. While the two of us floated lazily on our inflatables, Jeff looked over at me and said, "Eric, I don't get it. I don't understand how you have all these businesses, yet you're in my pool right now relaxing. Who's running your companies?"

At the time, I still ran Square 2 Marketing as one of the digital marketing agency's co-founders (along with the foreword's author, Mike Lieberman) as well as another marketing agency. I had a small software company. I also owned a commercial building in Philadelphia's historic downtown that housed a few upstairs apartments as well as my pizza shop (Big Ass Slices), bar (Silence Dogood's Tavern), and pedicycle tour company (Big Red Pedal Tours) on the ground floor.

I said to him, "Well, that's what being an entrepreneur is all about, right? You set up a business, you put the systems in place, you hire the right people, and then you let them do their jobs. I'm making money right now while I'm hanging out with you in your pool."

He laughed and shook his head.

A few weeks later, he called me up. "Eric," he said, "I can't stop thinking about what you said, about how you were making money while you were swimming in my pool. That's amazing."

It was almost a foreign concept to him. Jeff is a smart guy and a hard worker, but he's always put his talents to use as an employee. Great income, great job security. Good career. But the idea of making money while seemingly doing nothing did not compute.

He'd caught the entrepreneurial bug.

It was perfect timing for me. The woman who managed the bar and my pizzeria as well as the pedal pub business had a baby due in four months. I knew I either had to find someone capable of filling in for her or step in as the temporary manager myself. But like most entrepreneurs, I don't like the day-to-day stuff. I like to have an idea, figure it out, build the business, put the right team in place, develop effective processes, see it succeed, and then go find another challenge.

I offered to sell my brother-in-law Big Ass Slices and Big Red Pedal Tours. He said, "I'll take them."

We worked out a great deal and he became a business owner who succeeded despite COVID over the next couple of years.

Owning a Job vs. Owning a System

Robert Kiyosaki (a.k.a. "Rich Dad") says that most self-employed people don't actually own a business. They own a job. If they don't show up for work, nothing happens. This is true not only for mom-and-pop restaurants but lawyers, doctors, and accountants.

If a lawyer can't go into work, they can't bill for any hours worked. They might own their own practice but they still have to show up at the office like any other employee.

Kiyosaki marks the difference between entrepreneurs and the self-employed. Entrepreneurs have businesses that run on their own. They can take a day, a week, or a month off work and have nothing go wrong. In the words of another small business guru, Michael Gerber, true entrepreneurs work *on* their business, not just in it.

Entrepreneurs build a machine that consistently, predictably, and profitably manufactures the same widgets day after day. It doesn't matter whether that "widget" is a funeral service, painting a house, tax audits, or opening a new bank account. They have a proven process.

No business can scale without systems. If you spend more than five minutes inside any large organization, you'll run into a system. Granted, those systems may be incredibly inefficient (have you ever tried to talk to a customer service representative from your cell phone provider?) but they're there.

Scale = systems.

When Mike and I founded Square 2 Marketing, we knew this. From the very start, we tried to turn everything we did into a step-by-step process, from how we hired team members to paying the bills to delivering clients their marketing assets. But after several years, we hit a plateau of about $8 million in revenue. No matter what we did, our revenue stayed flat. This was particularly embarrassing for the owners of a marketing firm that prided itself on increasing client revenue.

I started talking to some of my entrepreneur buddies about being stuck. "We just can't seem to break through this ceiling." One of them asked if I'd ever read *Traction*. I said I hadn't, but I would put it on my to-do list.

Then another buddy asked if I'd read *Traction*. Then another asked if I heard about the Entrepreneurial Operating System (EOS).

Seeing as how so many entrepreneurs I respected were saying the same thing, I downloaded it on my Kindle and read through *Traction*, learning about EOS. It hit me like a ton of bricks: Mike and I had systems in place for everything inside the company. What we didn't have was a unified framework to run the entire company.

The Entrepreneurial Operating System®

EOS identifies six key components of every business.

1. Vision: Where is the business going and what's the plan to get there?

2. People: Are the right people in the right seats?

3. Data: Can we follow the metrics to know what we're doing works?

4. Issues: What are the main problems, obstacles, and challenges we need to clear?

5. Process: How do we document our core processes and get them followed by all?

6. Traction: Is everyone pulling in the same direction and helping execute the plan?

Mike and I had spent countless hours on our processes—but it was just one element of the six. No wonder we weren't getting traction in our business!

We found the EOS Implementer® for our area. We followed the EOS methodology religiously. In short order, everything started to get better. Over the next two years, margins doubled.

Profits tripled. Employee turnover went away. Client satisfaction was never higher. We were making more money than ever *and working less than ever.*

I was floored. When I got ready to retire, I offered Mike to buy me out. I decided I wanted to give back to the entrepreneurial community which had invested so much in me over the years, so I decided to become an EOS Implementer® myself. While I've taken on far too many EOS clients to say, "I'm retired" with a straight face, I love it.

Enhancing EOS®

There was one thing, though, while our EOS Implementer® was taking Mike and me through the implementation for Square 2. When we came to the marketing part, the conversation went something like this.

> *Implementer: "Okay, who's your perfect client?"*
>
> *Us: "Frank."*
>
> *Implementer: "Okay, tell me about Frank."*
>
> *Us: "Well, Frank's a good man. He pays his bills on time. He takes our advice. He's the owner of a company that wants to go from good to great."*
>
> *Implementer: "Great! Where are the Franks of the world located?"*
>
> *Us: "We work with anyone, really, but most of the 'Franks' of the world are here in the US."*
>
> *Implementer: "Now, why is Frank your best customer?"*

Us: "Well, because he pays his bills on time?"

Implementer: "Okay, last question. What are your 3 Uniques? What are three things you can use to validate why Frank should do business with Square 2?"

After we went through the exercise of identifying those, our Implementer said, "Great! Okay, that's it for marketing. Let's move on . . ."

Mike and I looked at each other. With our combined decades of marketing experience, it felt like we had barely scratched the surface. The 3 Uniques aligned with our focus on differentiating your company by being remarkable, but I knew that the vast majority of leadership teams going through an EOS rollout would give the same answers as the entrepreneurs in my seminars: "We have the best prices, we have the best people, we have X years in business." If everybody says that, then there's not a difference! At least, not a difference in their prospect's perception, which is all that matters.

Three years later when I became an EOS Implementer®, I felt that I couldn't just leave my clients with identifying a target customer, a geographic market, and identifying three things to validate working with us and then move on. Because it gnawed at me for all these sessions, I decided to do something about it and create the Alchemyze process to help people I know and, more importantly, help people I don't know take their marketing and differentiation to the next level. The other thing is EOS revolves around scaling. And if you don't have a sound marketing and/or sales strategy, no matter how good your plan, processes, or people are, you're still not going to be able to scale easily. You need to sell enough to get to the next level. And that's where the Alchemyze process will really throw a little gasoline on the fire.

I love the fact that EOS is all about scaling, but it just lightly brushes over the marketing strategy. An effective marketing strategy and specifically a killer differentiation strategy is how we're going to attract new people, get them into our database, tell our story, and sell them something again and again for years to come to build a bigger business. And if you have a weak strategy that's a huge gap.

As a professional marketer, I felt like I would be doing my clients a disservice. I had to not only facilitate them implementing EOS at their company but give them the tools they needed to differentiate themselves in their market.

That's where Alchemyze comes in.

And while the catalyst comes from wanting to enhance EOS's marketing exercise, it hits more than one of the core processes (including marketing, sales, operations, and customer retention) and even more than one of the key elements (including vision, data, and issues).

How?

Glad you asked.

3

You're Unique.
Just Like Everyone Else.

"Be a flamingo in a flock of pigeons."

—Unknown

One year, I dressed up as Ben Franklin for Halloween. I'm a Philly native and love all things liberty. The name of one of my businesses is Junto Consulting Group, a nod to Ben Franklin's Junto, a community group he founded when he was only 21. But after Halloween, I put my costume up and went back to being Eric Keiles.

I put on a mask for the night. It didn't change who I was. I acted the part, but nobody mistook me for the real Franklin. (Unlike that episode of *The Office* where Dwight can't decide whether to believe a Ben Franklin impersonator is actually Ben Franklin or not.) It was a temporary role.

Most companies, big or small, use marketing like a Halloween mask. They may put up a false front, but a new logo, expensive branding, or pouring money into advertising doesn't change what they truly are. You can pay a PR firm to reinvent your public image without changing anything about your company at all.

You might remember back in the early 2000s, the decades-old multi-level-marketing company Amway felt its name had too much baggage and rebranded itself as Quixtar. Nothing about the company had fundamentally changed. It was still an MLM, still relied on recruiting people as its fundamental business model, and still sold essentially the same line of products. In fact, the company switched back to the Amway name just a decade later, spending millions in advertising dollars to let everyone know it was the same company it had been all along.

I think my favorite example is Domino's. I don't have to ask you what Domino's sells. You know it sells pizza. But the same year Quixtar switched back to Amway, Domino's Pizza dropped the pizza and rebranded itself simply as "Domino's." The idea was to signal to the world that the company sold more than just pizza. They sold pasta and chicken wings, too. Nothing about the company changed. All these years later, Domino's still stands for pizza.

Now, let me talk to you for a moment about marketing *strategy*. A marketing strategy isn't putting on a Halloween mask for a day. It's about your identity. Who and what you are. Why you do what you do.

Marketing Tactics vs. Marketing Strategy

I once worked with an accounting firm in the heart of Philadelphia. They had about seventy employees altogether working out of a high-rise office building. They did great work at a great price with great people and great customer service . . . just like the dozens of other accounting firms in Philly.

What was different about them?

The first clue in the Alchemyze process is to ask, "Who's your perfect client?"

After a little digging, I found that their ideal client was someone who had lots of problems with the IRS, often because they had a complex set of businesses and assets. They didn't file correctly, their returns were a tax code nightmare, whatever. Their taxes were overwhelming and the IRS was gunning for them. These accountants loved making sure their clients didn't pay a penny more than they were legally obligated to.

They became the *Tax Warriors*. Their mission became fighting Uncle Sam on behalf of their clients. On the surface, they still provided the exact same services. But as the Tax Warriors, they saw themselves as having a unified mission. Yes, they would continue to provide other accounting services, but being the Tax Warriors became their mission, their rallying cry. It completely separated them from all the other accountants in Greater Philadelphia. It gave them a new identity and a new purpose.

Where their competitors spent money advertising (putting on a Halloween mask), the Tax Warriors Alchemyzed their business (reinventing themselves). That's the difference between marketing and a marketing strategy.

They became a flamingo in a flock of pigeons.

Seth Godin's *Purple Cow* may be more than 20 years old, but his advice is timeless. If you go for a ride out in the country, soon you will drive past some brown cows. They more or less all look the same. After a while, you don't even notice the cows because there is nothing that interesting about just another brown cow. But if one of those cows is painted purple, that's the one you focus on. It stands out from the crowd. I've preached Godin's advice for years, but after some thought, I think it's deeper than being a different color. It's about being fundamentally different. A flamingo in a flock of pigeons.

Take Warby Parker, for example. If you've worn glasses for years, you might remember going to the old-timey optometrist's office. After going to a dark room and getting your vision checked ("Better one or better two?"), you were led into another dark room filled with rows of dusty eyeglasses. Although you couldn't see because your eyes were still dilated, the assistant led you to a particular section and told you that your insurance would cover these frames. While you might not have really liked the selection they had, that's what you were stuck with. You picked your least hated pair and then waited weeks for your custom eyeglasses to come in.

Warby Parker changed all that. Although they still technically compete with traditional optometrists, the difference is daylight and dark. If you go to their retail stores, it's like walking into an Apple Store. Clean, bright, and light. You can go online, order five frames from their overwhelming selection, and have them shipped to your door. I love it. All for $95 a pop. For me, Warby Parker is the obvious choice.

That's the key—being the *obvious* choice.

I call it being remarkable.

What It Means to Be Remarkable

To be remarkable, you need two things:

1. To offer something so unique . . .

2. That your customer tells someone else.

If your customer is able to make a positive remark to someone else, you are literally remark-able.

If you've been in business for more than three years, believe me: You are doing something remarkable. If you didn't, you wouldn't still be in business! Your problem is that you're too close to the problem. With most of my clients, I find they have a fantastic inner reality that they fail to translate into outside perception. If you can get those two aligned—like to have a stress-free office buildout or being passionate about defending against the IRS—revenue goes through the roof.

That's what Alchemyze is all about: taking something ordinary (to you) and turning it into something remarkable (to everyone else). Alchemyze is a marketing differentiation strategy. You use a proven process to create a strategy to show the world how your company is uniquely unique.

In the early days before Square 2 Marketing took off, Mike and I would practice for hours. We would drive up and down Route 611 in Philly quizzing each other on how to make ordinary businesses remarkable.

> Me: "How do you make a mom-and-pop bakery remarkable? Go!"
>
> Mike: "HUGE muffins. Flavors from every continent. A different pastry from a different country every week."

We've come a long way from those days. Serving "yuge" muffins or putting a larger-than-life donut on top of the building are really gimmicks. But that's the thing. Even gimmicks are sometimes enough to make you stand out.

The small business marketing guru Dan Kennedy told the story about the guy who was an auto parts distributor. Every quarter or so, he would send out an enormous printout of all his available products. So did all the other guys. After going to a Dan Kennedy seminar, the only thing the distributor could come up with to stand out was to print his catalog on neon pink paper.

And that was enough.

Sales rose significantly just because he gave his customers a reason to choose him over the others. What does using neon pink paper have to do with being the best auto parts distributor? Nothing. But if everyone looks exactly the same, even something as crazy as your paper color helps you stand out.

Alchemyze is deeper than some gimmick, but my point here is that your customers are looking for a reason—any reason—to help them decide who to use. Don't let them flip a coin. Give them an excuse to choose you. Be different. Solve their problems.

Now, let's do a deeper dive on how to transform your pigeon into a flamingo.

4

The Alchemyze Process

"In marketing, I've seen only one strategy that can't miss—and that is to market to your best customers first, your best prospects second, and the rest of the world third."

—JOHN ROMERO, DIGITAL GAME DESIGNER

EOS is an amazing system. It's the focal point of my professional life here in the "sunset" stage of my career. But after our implementer walked us through the marketing exercise of Square 2's EOS implementation, Mike and I were sorely disappointed. EOS gave us everything we were missing. We could take our marketing and differentiation strategy further from our own experience. Not everyone can do that.

Alchemyze It!

I once worked with a landscaping company in Baton Rouge, Louisiana, called Lion's Landscaping. I started the meeting off with the owners—Luis and Ulysses—by putting myself in their customer's shoes. If I own a home and want someone to take care of the outside, who should I call? Should I use a big company (that might be more expensive)? Should I use a smaller company (that might not be reliable)? Should I hire the two guys in a truck going around the neighborhood (who may or may not show up next month)? It's confusing.

When I posed the question, "Why should I use Lion's?" I heard what I hear all too often: "We have been in business more than 15 years. We carry all the proper licenses and insurance. We have experience working in landscaping of all types. If you don't know what you want, we can design your landscaping. We're a small company, so we get involved with every project."

They do great work. The before-and-after pictures on their professionally designed website attest to the quality of their work. They're not the most expensive, but they're not the rock-bottom cheapest, either. They can do just about anything landscaping-related you want. But how can they stand out from the flock of pigeons serving Greater Baton Rouge?

I said, "When I ran a digital marketing firm, typically what happened is that people would come to us and say, 'We need more leads.' We would ask them, 'Okay . . . but do you really want more leads? Or do you want more revenue?' Of course, they say revenue. That's what businesses are really after, right? So, I then ask them what their sales close rate is. They might say they close two out of every ten sales meetings. A 20% close rate is fine. But instead of feeding the top of the sales funnel—by putting more leads in the top—what if they could just close just two extra deals out of every ten opportunities? That would take their close rate from 20% to 40%, effectively doubling their revenue without spending a dime in extra advertising dollars."

Of course, that was music to Luis's and Ulysses's ears.

Step 1: BHAG

If you're an entrepreneur who loves to dream about the future, it might come as a surprise to you that most business owners rarely think about putting "a dent in the universe," as Steve Jobs so famously said. They're mostly worried about keeping all the plates spinning, hoping sales covers payroll that week. Few think about what they could achieve in five or ten years. Fewer still have a ten-year plan.

Popularized in his book *Built to Last*, Jim Collins created what is called "A Big Hairy Audacious Goal." It's a compelling, long-term goal that is intriguing enough to inspire your employees to take action. The term is abbreviated as BHAG, which is pronounced "bee-hag." It serves as a "north star" to help guide your team's decision-making.

The purpose of a BHAG is to get everyone "rowing in the same direction," "singing off the same sheet," "marching to the same beat," or however you want to say it. The idea is the same: get everyone's efforts aligned. With a single focus, everyone can become single-minded.

Step 2: Persona

I said, "Okay, let's figure out who loves working with you already, and we're going to do that with a little reverse engineering. Tell me the name of your favorite client, someone you really enjoyed working with."

It didn't take long for Luis and Ulysses to come up with the name of Keith.

"Why?"

Keith doesn't use Lion's Landscaping for his lawn maintenance. He's done multiple landscaping projects with Lions. And that's where Luis and Ulysses really make their money. Lawn care is a commodity business which means thin profit margins. Custom design and installation work—*that's* where the real money is. But the reason they like working with Keith isn't because they've made more money off him than their average customer.

He's their perfect customer because ". . . he knows what he wants," Luis told me. "He is very open-minded when it comes to budgeting. He's not afraid to spend more to get what he really wants. I love his property. It's not mine, but I feel a sense of ownership with his house because we've done so much of the design and installation work. He appreciates the value of good landscaping. He understands that a project isn't a one-time thing. It requires annual maintenance to keep it looking good from season to season. He also refers his friends and family to our firm."

"And how is he different from some of your other clients?" I asked.

"Well, with some of them, you have to educate them on the importance of doing maintenance work. If you spend six grand to clean up your landscaping but don't do anything after that, next year you'll have to spend six grand again because you let it go. Keith takes great pride in how his home looks, always."

"If you could surround yourself with more Keiths," I said, "would you be a happier camper? If most of your customers were just like Keith, would that transform your business? Would that add some serious rocket fuel to Lion's Landscaping?"

Of course it would.

"So, the purpose of your marketing is to find more Keiths. Keith becomes Lion's 'persona,' the person who represents your ideal customer. When Luis says, 'Hey, I've got three Keiths lined up,' Ulysses knows exactly what he's talking about. The next time your crew goes to Keith's house, get a picture of him and hang it in the conference room. That sounds a little creepy but his picture is an ever-present reminder that Keith needs to be part of every conversation. Lion's Landscaping is on a mission to serve the Keiths of Greater Baton Rouge. That's what your company does. That's who you are."

EOS is on the right track in getting entrepreneurs and business leaders to identify a target customer and a geographic market. After all, Lion's Landscaping couldn't help a "Keith" who lives in Philadelphia. It makes sense to identify that they provide services for Greater Baton Rouge. But you need to take it one step further. You need to know your target customer's demographics.

"Geographic" means to define the geography of your target customer, a.k.a. the "where." "Demographic" means to define the "what" of your target customer. What's their age? What's their income? What's their education? What's their gender?

You can get as specific as makes sense for your business. For Lion's Landscaping, the Keiths of Baton Rouge are:

- homeowners
- married
- established in their careers, so 30's to 60's
- affluent

That's really about as detailed as Lion's needs to get.

Then there's one last thing to think about. What are Keith's psychographics? If "geographic" means to define their geography, "psychographic" means to define their psychology. In other words, this is the "why." Why are they your favorite client? How do they think? What makes them tick? What's important to them?

Luis and Ulysses already knew Keith's psychographics:

- getting what he wants is more important than price—he's value-oriented
- landscaping isn't a one-and-done but an ongoing project—relationships
- budgets for landscaping throughout the year—plays the longer game

- decisive yet open-minded and collaborative—appreciates advice
- values long-term relationships—wants a partner, not just a vendor

Psychographics is the missing piece. If we went strictly by Keith's demographics, Lion's would try to market to just about every house in every subdivision with above-average incomes. But some of those houses are owned by Baby Boomers raised by parents who lived in Louisiana during the Great Depression. Their parents taught them to be more frugal. Beautiful landscaping isn't as important to them as saving every penny they can.

Knowing Keith as we do now, what kind of marketing would attract Keith? Definitely not messages about being the cheapest in town. Getting good value is important to everyone, but people like Keith don't want the cheapest guys. Keith wants the best.

Showcasing customers who have been with Lion's for years with multiple projects. Talking about a collaborative approach to custom designs. Specials when the customer combines a project with annual maintenance. Those types of messages would appeal to Keith.

Those things are the beginnings of nailing down Lion's persona. Next up: Keith's core problems.

Step 3: Core Problems

Hear me now: no purchase is ever made unless it makes a pain or problem go away. Think about that for a second. If that's the case, your job is to demonstrate that your company can make those pains and problems disappear.

So, what worries Keith when it comes to his landscaping? Luis and Ulysses's right-hand person, Adriana, spoke up.

"One thing that has been a challenge for us is consistency. We're a seasonal business, so we lose a lot of our workers during the off season. In the spring, although we have a lot of our same guys come back, we also get a lot of new employees and they don't always do things the way the crew did last year. So, we try to send out the same crew to Keith's every time."

I said, "Perfect. Consistency. He wants to know he's going to get what he expects. And I imagine that's true when it comes to his landscaping projects, too, right? He wants to make sure you guys make good on the vision he has in mind?"

"Yes. For instance, when we design for a six-foot tree, we have to make sure he understands that we don't plant a six-foot tree. We plant something small that will grow to be six feet," Adriana said.

"What about time and budget?"

"With Keith, we've never really had that problem because he plans ahead so well. But with other customers, yes. Someone may contact us and say they need landscaping done for a Mother's Day gift. Sometimes we can do that, but sometimes it's a crazy short timeline."

I said, "Luis talked about educating your customers. Is that something you do often?"

She said, "Yes, that too. Plenty of people don't know what grows well in Louisiana or what types of plants are low maintenance versus very time-consuming. We spend a lot of time helping people understand what's best for their yard and their lifestyle."

In just a few minutes, Adriana identified five of Keith's core problems:

1. Inconsistency from season to season

2. His vision matching the outcome

3. Reality of what's planted versus what he expected to be planted

4. Hitting deadlines

5. Needing to be educated so they're happy in the long run

We identified Lion's persona. We identified their persona's core problems. Step four is identifying solutions to those core problems.

Step 4: Solutions

The solution to pain point #1 could be to set up a training process so Lion's workers consistently deliver the same quality, regardless of who's working. "Process" is a basic tenet of EOS. Perhaps they could institute a quarterly training program. Maybe the workers who return the next season could be supervisors or quality control people. Maybe the first two weeks a new person is hired, they shadow an experienced worker like a helper or apprentice would. Whatever Lion's decides on, that's an internal process.

It seems to me that numbers 2, 3, and 5, are really about communication. As part of their client onboarding process—and throughout their delivery—Lion's needs to budget adequate time to speak with the customer.

But hitting deadlines . . . what's the solution there?

This is a good time to talk about your 3 Uniques.

In Traction, *Gino Wickman shares the example of Southwest Airlines' 3 Uniques: low fares, lots of flights, and loads of fun. While other airlines might be able to also claim one of those things, I've never flown an airline that could claim all three of those.*

Most business leaders have a knee-jerk reaction to creating a persona. They believe they're leaving money on the table by purposely ignoring a huge part of their potential market. The truth is you can't be all things to all people. That's a recipe for disaster. Walmart can't compete with dollar stores and Tiffany's at the same time. You have to pick a lane.

Southwest stays in its lane. After introducing Southwest's 3 Uniques, Gino said that one frequent flier wrote a complaint letter after every flight. She complained about the lack of first-class, the cattle-call seating, how informal and casual everyone was, no meals being served, and just about every way that Southwest was different from normal airlines.

She complained so often that one of her letters eventually made its way to the CEO's desk, founder Herb Kelleher.

He simply wrote back, "Dear Mrs. Crabapple, we will miss you. Love, Herb"[1]

Herb Kelleher is legendary for his focus on customer service. He wasn't being sarcastic. He wasn't being mean. He simply knew she wasn't Southwest's persona.

"The 3 Uniques" is slightly misleading. In EOS, the combination of the three characteristics is what makes the company unique—not that each of those traits is unique by themselves. I get that, but I think we can take it a step further. Instead of three things you do that *together* set your company apart, I want you to have an inventory of solutions that are *each* remarkable in themselves. As you might guess, I call these "Remarkables."

What are the remarkable ways Lion's Landscaping could solve Keith's pains? I'll share just one we came up with.

"When someone calls up Lion's Landscaping and says they want some landscaping, what happens?" I asked the trio.

---

1 Gino Wickman, *Traction: Get a Grip on Your Business* (Dallas: BenBella Books, 2011), 60.

Adriana spoke up for the group. "We tell them we'd love to help them. The first thing we do is get some information and then connect them with one of our estimators. He will come out to their house and have a discussion about what your needs are, and we'll go from there. Sometimes there's some back and forth, sometimes it's about the price. Then we follow up with them, take the down payment, and schedule the project."

I said, "While that's 100% accurate, let's be honest. Is that something that's going to make someone go, 'Wow! Someone's going to come to my house and talk to me!' That's not very remarkable, is it? So, how can we make it remarkable? Let's take what you just said and reframe it in a remarkable way. Luis and Ulysses, you guys came up with the idea of a lion as the symbol for your company, so let's use that theme."

I continued, "The next time someone calls Lion's, here's what I would say:

> *Thank you so much for the opportunity to work with you. Did one of our customers refer you? What was their name? Eric Keiles? Eric is one of our favorite clients, and any friend of Eric's is a friend of ours. Let me share with you the proprietary, five-step process we've developed over the 15 years we've been in business called L.I.O.N.S., L-I-O-N-S:*

> - *L for listen: We want to learn about your priorities on this initial phone call. What's important to you and what your goals are.*

> - *I for imagine: An expert from our design lab will come to your home and, together, the two of you will imagine what your home could look like.*

> - *O for optimize: Our expert will return here to our design lab and determine how to best make your vision come to life with your budget, schedule, and other constraints.*

- *N for navigate: Our experienced crew will come build and install your project using plants from our local nursery, ensuring you have everything you need to bring your landscaping to life, navigating through all the details and logistics involved.*

- *S for sustain: Your design lab expert will return to your home every 90 days for the first year to ensure everything is growing and getting cared for like you originally envisioned.*

"Now," I said to the three, "which landscaping company is Keith going to remember? The other two guys who said they'll send an estimator to your house and come back to you with a quote? Or Lion's Landscaping who has their proprietary five-step L.I.O.N.S. process for delivering on their dream yard? Which of these three companies offers something remarkable? And the beauty is you already do this! There's just a better way to tell your story."

For the sake of time, I won't walk you through the other two Remarkables we created for Lion's, but you get the idea. Whether it's something you already do (like sending out a punch-list manager or your SOP for product delivery) or something new you create (some examples of which I'm about to show you), you need Remarkables that solve your prospects' core problems in such an interesting way that it gives them something to talk about when telling others about using your company.

Step 5: The Big Story

Step five of Alchemyze is to create the big story. This isn't really Lion's Landscaping's story. Remember, marketing is about attracting your persona. This is Keith's story. Luis and Ulysses had multiple motivations for starting Lion's, and they have an incredible story of overcoming the odds to do it . . . but does Keith really care about the owners' hardships? Keith sounds like a decent guy, so he probably would care a little. But he cares a *lot* more about solving his core problems. As Luis said, "Our clients are very important to us. We want every family to have a beautiful home."

Now, that's a story that speaks to Keith. By calling it out and making it the company's Big Story, it focuses everyone in the company not on selling landscaping but on "helping families make their homes beautiful." Lion's Landscaping is on a mission to create a beautiful home for every family.

Remember the safety products provider? Their big story is "Getting Everyone Home Safely Each Night." That really connects emotionally with safety officers and warehouse managers who lie awake in bed each night worrying that a team member will get hurt on their shift.

Once you pull everything together, make sure you always present your story with the "newspaper approach." Think about a newspaper article. The first thing that grabs your attention is the headline. Next comes the most important information about the article; the meat, if you will. At the end of the article are all the little details. Think: Head first, body second, tail last. Start with your headline (from step 6 which you're about to read). Then relate the meat of your story. Put the details at the tail.

Step 6: Headline

Alchemyze step six is to encapsulate everything you can do for a prospect or client in one phrase that emotionally connects with them, a.k.a. a Headline. Something that could be used on the homepage's banner, the subject line of an email, your salesperson's opening sentence, or the main line of a Google ad. The four of us tossed around some ideas like "On a mission to make Baton Rouge's homes beautiful" or "Beautify Baton Rouge."

Let's dig a little deeper into each of the Alchemyze steps.

5

Why Before What: The BHAG

"Shoot for the moon. Even if you miss, you'll land among the stars."

—APOCRYPHAL

"Impossible."

That's the very word people have used the first time someone wanted to try something new. The Wright brothers' dream to invent an airplane. Charles Lindbergh's nonstop flight across the Atlantic. Roger Bannister running a four-minute mile. Chuck Yeager breaking the sound barrier. The Apollo moon landing.

Yet today, these are everyday events. Okay, maybe not landing on the moon. But that's only because of how expensive it is. But it won't be long before even that is common. I mean, who could have dreamed that we would have *space tourists!?* Yet we have Elon Musk's SpaceX, Richard Branson's Virgin Galactic, and Jeff Bezos's Blue Origin doing exactly that.

Anytime someone says they want to do something that's never been done, you'll find plenty of people who say it can't be done at all. When President John F. Kennedy announced his plan in 1961 to put a man on the moon—and safely bring him back—before the end of the decade, many thought it was a publicity stunt. It was physically impossible . . . wasn't it?

That's where we get the term "moonshot" from. It's a crazy goal that seems impossible. But JFK wasn't crazy. He was a visionary. His dream motivated an entire nation to dream big and do things humanly impossible. And though he didn't live to see it, he achieved his moonshot with a few months to spare. On July 20, 1969, Neil Armstrong stepped out of the Apollo lunar module and onto the surface of the moon.

The EOS Vision/Traction Organizer (or V/TO) is necessary, but it isn't what we'd call emotionally connecting. It's mostly meant to be an internal document, but your marketing and differentiation strategy has to connect with external stakeholders like prospects and clients.

As EOS Worldwide puts it:

"Usually, businesses devote a lot of time and resources to assigning committees to work on different sections of their business strategy. This frequently leads to the production of long 50-to-100-page documents which sometimes aren't joined up with the big picture or aren't simple to communicate.

The V/TO is unique because it organizes both the Vision Component™ of your business and includes your plan to make that vision a reality."

For more, see
www.eosworldwide.com/blog/whats-in-your-v-to

The V/TO is essential. It's logical. It's logistical. But it's a bit lacking.

It doesn't have the power to unite people. It doesn't tell everyone *what* they're really doing. It doesn't say *why* they're doing it.

The marketing component of the V/TO needs some oomph, if you will.

I ask you . . . what's your moonshot?"

What's your big hairy audacious goal? What's the dream? What is all this for?

To Fight for the Working Poor

I'll give you a beautiful example. I once worked with Hudson River Community Credit Union, about an hour north of Albany, New York, in the Adirondack Mountains. We started working through this exercise.

First, I had them choose a date. The V/TO has the 3-Year Picture and the 10-Year Target, but for this, I let my clients choose the timeline. Do they want to talk about what they can do in five years? Twenty years? What can their company do in one hundred years? It doesn't matter. We set a date because otherwise it's a moving target, and it's a lot harder to hit a moving target. HRCCU chose five years.

I said, "Next up, what do you want your revenue and profits to be in five years?"

They settled on an ambitious but reachable number.

Finally, they needed to pick their "measurable."

"What's a measurable? It's a way to track how you're moving the ball down the field. Typically, leadership teams choose 'profit' or 'revenue' as their measurable, such as 'We want to reach $3 million in profit in five years.' What's a metric you can follow—aside from profit itself—that tells you you're on the right track?" I asked.

That opened up a fascinating line of questions. The obvious answer for a community credit union is the number of members. But when I asked them how many more members they could get, we ran into a wall. Hudson River was such an important part of its four-county area that virtually *every* person was already a member. They thought they could pick up a few hundred more. Certainly not enough to achieve their goals.

I said, "Okay, well, getting more members around here isn't the answer, then. Do you see yourselves expanding throughout eastern New York? Going across the state line to Vermont?"

While growing bigger was a logical path, no one seemed all that excited about it.

"If it's not about growing bigger or getting more members, then what's it all about? What's the whole reason for Hudson River? Why do you guys work here?" I wasn't being confrontational. I wanted to understand the shared but unspoken *why* behind their efforts.

One woman spoke up. "Really, we just want to help our existing members." She went on to talk about how 92% of their members lived at or below the poverty line. They all felt that a big part of their job was to help the people in their community.

The traditional banks like Wells Fargo or Bank of America were purely numbers-driven. They had no interest in serving people who had next to nothing in their accounts. They didn't care about improving the lives of people there.

I said, "What if you could move a third of your members above the poverty line? What would that look like?"

Everyone started talking at once. Energy and enthusiasm filled the conference room. I watched as their faces almost literally brightened at the idea of lifting their working poor members out of poverty.

I said, "There you go. That's your moonshot."

We formalized it like this:

By December 31, 2029,
Hudson River Community Credit Union
will reduce the percentage of its members
at or below the poverty line from 92% to 67%.

To lift almost a third of the surrounding area's population out of poverty? In just five years? That's an insane number. That seems like an impossible mission. That sounds like crazy talk.

That's a moonshot.

Maybe they don't make it. But that's not the purpose of a moonshot. At least, not for my clients. The whole idea is to make sure everyone has the same vision. In *Traction*, Gino talks about a tech company stuck for two years. They identified their lack of a central vision. By using the V/TO, they settled on one direction. To focus, they had to completely stop offering two of their three core services.

Many business owners can't imagine saying no to money. How can you make more money by dropping money makers? If the two services were profitable, it didn't make any sense to stop selling them. But it worked. At the time of Gino's writing, the company had just had its best-ever first quarter at an astounding 125% increase over the previous year's.

One BHAG to Rule Them All?

When you think about your BHAG, you have to ask a question. Have you ever heard a teacher tell their students, "Okay, let's use our 'inside' voices now!" It's okay to be loud when they're running around on the playground. But in the classroom, they need to turn the volume down.

When you come up with your BHAG, you need to decide if it works for both the "inside" and the "outside." Hudson River's

BHAG is wonderful because it works inside the organization as well as outward facing. Whether interviewing a potential employee or posting on social media, everyone can get excited about lifting people out of poverty. But that's not always the case.

I worked with a pest control company in New Jersey one time. I asked the owner what the dream was. He said, "I want to double the size of the company and sell it to Terminix." That was his BHAG. That was at the back of his mind on all his decisions. He operated out of that vision.

I said, "Got it. Now, unfortunately, that's not going to work for anyone else."

He seemed surprised. "Why?"

"Well," I said, "when you talk about doubling the size of the company and selling it, the only thing everybody else hears is that you're going to get rich. That's exciting for you, but that doesn't inspire anybody else. If I went to your website and read that that's the reason you do what you do, I won't emotionally connect with that."

He shrugged. "I don't know what to tell you. That's what I'm doing here."

"Let's translate your goal into something everybody inside and outside the company can get behind. You told me earlier your average customer spends $1,000 a year on pest control. If you want to double your company to $10 million, then you need ten thousand customers. Right?"

"Right . . . "

"So a BHAG that you *and* everyone inside and outside your company can get behind would be to rid 10,000 New Jersey homes of pests."

Do you see how that works? It's fine if your primary goal in your business is financial success. That's capitalism. Nothing wrong with that. Becoming a millionaire, retiring early, and creating generational wealth is very motivating . . . for you. But your BHAG has to get other people excited, too.

In the Alchemyze workbook, do "Step #2: What's a BHAG?"

6

Persona

***

"I can't give you a surefire formula for success, but I can give you a formula for failure: try to please everybody all the time."

—Herbert Bayard Swope

Poor Mary. Even at the end of her life, she denied ever killing anyone.

But she did. At least five people that we know of. She put scores of people in the hospital and put thousands of others at risk. Historians believe that because she used a number of aliases, her death toll could be higher. Some knew her as Mary Brown. Others met her as Mary Breshof. She was born Mary Mallon.

You might remember her as Typhoid Mary.

Patient Zero. A natural carrier of typhoid fever yet also naturally immune to it. She spread the disease wherever she went. (Even after doctors proved this, she refused to believe it.) There were multiple outbreaks around Manhattan and Long Island in the early 1900s, many directly traced back to Mary. Everything started with her.

While I certainly hope your customers don't get sick, you need to identify your own "client zero." In marketing terms, the "persona." Everything starts with them. You're trying to create viral marketing. You want who and what you are to spread to the four corners of the earth. Or at least the county.

Why is it so important to identify your perfect client?

Because that's your real market.

Your Target Customer vs. Your Real Customer

Your business isn't just about what you sell. It's about the *way* you sell it.

There are plenty of business examples of companies that started selling one product, only to find out their main customer was someone else completely. Take WD-40. If your dad did anything in the garage, he had a can of WD-40. Great to spray on stuck bolts or to protect bicycle chains from rusting or to get door hinges to stop squeaking.

Would you believe the inventors first made it for missiles?

In 1953, the Rocket Chemical Company wanted to create a water displacement substance (hence the "WD") to keep rockets and missile parts from seizing up. The employees at one aerospace customer liked WD-40 so much that they started sneaking cans out of the plant to use at home. Figuring there might be an opportunity there, the founder of Rocket Chemical put WD-40 in a spray can to see how it would do on store shelves around their hometown, San Diego, in 1958.

In less than two years, the company doubled in size. By 1969, the company renamed itself WD-40. An estimated four out of every five households in the US currently have a can of it sitting around somewhere.

It didn't matter that the company thought its customers were aerospace contractors and Uncle Sam. It turned out that its true customer was a DIY homeowner. Its perfect client wasn't even someone on its radar.

The gum maker Wrigley? Originally manufactured soap and baking soda. The company gave away chewing gum with its products as a promotional tool in the early 1900s. Realizing the public wanted the chewing gum more than the baking soda, the company reinvented itself. It's now the largest producer of chewing gum in the world.

These companies thought they were selling *this* product to *this* customer. Turns out, their best customer was someone else entirely. They didn't change their products to better fit their target customer. They changed their marketing to focus on people who were already a perfect fit for what they sold.

These are dramatic examples, but you get the point. Your company is perfect for a certain type of person. And maybe that person isn't who you'd expect.

What Lights Up Your Persona?

Mark Twain said the difference between the right word and the almost right word is the difference between lightning and a lightning bug. The same is true with your persona. Take Keith's neighbor, Karen. She's a married homeowner in a professional career with a great income living in an affluent neighborhood in Baton Rouge. She's the same age as Keith. They send their kids to the same school. At first glance, they seem to be the same or a similar persona.

But Karen is a *Karen*.

She doesn't have Keith's collaborative approach. She wants what she wants, and she wants it now. And she better get a discount for her inconvenience or she's talking to the manager! For

Lion's Landscaping, the customer of their dreams lives just one house away from their nightmare.

Do Luis, Ulysses, and Adriana want ten Keiths? Or ten Karens?

The difference between a light bulb and a laser is its degree of focus. By focusing on their perfect client, Lion's business could explode. Without focus—if they diffused their marketing—they might attract a lot of Karens on a mission to destroy the company. While every customer can't be a Keith and not every customer will be a Karen, wouldn't you like to have more of one and less of the other?

That's why getting your persona right is crucial.

Remember our friends at Hudson River Community Credit Union? As you might imagine, they had an enormous variety of people they served. If a business has vastly different divisions or product lines, sometimes it makes sense to have a persona for each one.

But HRCCU basically offered all the same services to their melting pot of customers. We decided to act like the credit union had four major segments and created a persona for each of them:

1. subpar credit families

2. seniors and their caretakers

3. local small business owners

4. school administrators

Here's the subpar credit persona:

Name: *Subpar Sam*

Demographic: *Ages 18–65. Independent; homeowner or renter. Employed, either fully or partially. Active/visible in the community.*

Geographic: *lives, works, worships, or studies in Saratoga, Warren, Washington, and/or Rensselaer counties*

Psychographic: Sam is looking for assistance from his financial institution since he struggles to make ends meet. He's not afraid of asking for help and is open-minded about learning how to improve his or his family's financial situation. He's often afraid, stressed, or worried about the future but is willing to make the effort to improve. He's happy to share the story of how HRCCU helped him or his family.

For their senior citizens:

Name: Mrs. Martha Mature

Demographic: Ages 65+. Semi-independent. Homeowner or renter. Retired.

Geographic: lives, works, worships, or studies in Saratoga, Warren, Washington, and/or Rensselaer counties

Psychographic: Martha trusts her financial institution. She is fearful of being taken advantage of via fraud or outright theft. She is somewhat lonely and looks at the HRCCU team as part of her world and often as her friends.

For small business owners:

Name: Emily the Entrepreneur

Demographic: Ages 25+. Owns a business of $2 million or less in revenue. Uses multiple offerings/services from HRCCU.

Geographic: lives, works, worships, or studies in Saratoga, Warren, Washington, and/or Rensselaer counties

Psychographic: Sheri needs a financial institution that understands how hard it is to balance her business and *personal life. She sometimes runs into challenges and often needs advice about how to handle her finances. She is open-minded and truly values the personal interactions she gets from her credit union. She was frustrated with larger traditional banks that treated her like a number. She's happy to share about her relationship with HRCCU to her fellow business owners and associates.*

For local school programs:

Name: *Scott the School Administrator*

Demographic: *A leader in a local school district who can make the decision to initiate an elementary student educational program in partnership with HRCCU.*

Geographic: *Schools located within Saratoga, Warren, Washington, and Rensselaer counties or the towns of Cohoes, Watervliet, or Green Island*

Psychographic: *Scott is constantly looking for ways to enhance the experience of his students. He is aligned with HRCCU's mission of helping the community exceed the poverty line and understands that financial education is a viable strategy to help. He is communicative and responsive and is willing to sing the praises of the student banking program with his local education colleagues in the community.*

Now, when HRCCU wants to offer a new product or service, they don't design it for the faceless masses. It has to serve Sam, Martha, Emily, or Scott. Throughout the company, there's no question of who the credit union sees as their customer. It's the struggling individuals in their community who need a financial institution they can turn to for help and trusted advice. Without knowing anything else about HRCCU, you can see their trajectory. They don't want to be the next Chase or Bank of America. They want to be an integral part of their community and their customers' lives.

Who Your Persona Isn't

Here's the flip side of why you need laser focus on your persona: You know who your customer is *not*. There's a great fictional conversation in Patrick Lencioni's book *Getting Naked*. (In case you're wondering, the title refers to being honest, transparent, and vulnerable with your customers. Wanted to clear up any misunderstanding right out of the gate.) The exchange between two characters reads like this:

> *Dick laughed too, "We've learned over the years that having a bad client is worse than having none."*
>
> *"How could that be if they're paying you?"*
>
> *Dick didn't have to think about it. "Well, for one, it prevents you from finding other good clients. And you're unlikely to get a good reference. In fact, they're likely to tell everyone they know how you weren't able to help them, because they certainly aren't going to admit it was their fault."*[2]

Let me emphasize that: **Having a bad client is worse than having none.** A good marketing differentiation strategy not only attracts the people who love working with a company like yours. It also repels people who would hate working with you. People who aren't a good fit for what you do and how you do it.

---

2 *Getting Naked: A Business Fable About Shedding the Three Fears That Sabotage Client Loyalty* by Patrick Lencioni

Take my writing partner for this book, Derek. Some ghostwriters interview the author, disappear into a cave for several months, then come out with a finished book. The author reads through it and the ghostwriter does a round of edits. Done.

If you're pressed for time and your content is straightforward, working with that kind of ghostwriter is great. Derek, on the other hand, has a collaborative approach with his authors (he calls it his Frankendraft process). His process starts off with a three-day "author retreat" that's half interview, half brainstorming session, and more than a little therapy. We worked closely together, often on a weekly basis. Each chapter he wrote started new conversations and shaped the chapters that followed. At the end of his third step, we went back and did a major overhaul of the entire manuscript. I spent hours not only talking and reading but writing and rewriting parts of the book. He loves for his authors to get their hands dirty.

If you want a book but don't want to spend a lot of time on it, Derek is not your guy. From the get-go, I knew I was going to be heavily involved. In his sales call, he walks prospects through his five-step Frankendraft process. It is not for the faint of heart. But for me, he's perfect.

Next up: What's wrong with them?

In the Alchemyze workbook, do "Step #3: Define Your Persona(s)."

7

What's That Feeling
They Can't Shake?

"In selling, as in medicine, prescription before diagnosis is malpractice."

—JIM CATHCART, *RELATIONSHIP SELLING*

R ead this next line carefully. Your business depends on it.

No one buys anything unless it solves their pain or problem.

Ever.

Name any product or service in any industry. I can show you how it fixes a problem or soothes their pain. Sometimes, the problem is obvious. If you're hungry, you need to eat. Unless you live on a farm, you have to buy food. But why do you buy some food from the grocery store but other food from Starbucks? Why does the same person who eats at Chili's sometimes go to Chez Quis[3]?

Different problems. Maybe you went to the grocery store because you're trying to save some money by making lunch at home. But when you have all-day meetings and don't have time to really eat, you might grab a pastry at Starbucks along with your coffee. You ate at Chili's because your customer suggested it and

---

3 Yes, that's a *Ferris Bueller's Day Off* joke.

you don't want to rock the boat. But if an anniversary is coming up, you need to let your significant other know how important they are to you. Reservation for two at Chez Quis, please.

Even luxury buys solve a problem. You don't pay thousands extra for a Louis Vuitton bag because it's better than every other leather purse out there. You can get better quality craftsmanship cheaper. But people recognize the distinctive "LV" on the bag. It's a status symbol. It solves an emotional pain.

Maybe that pain is low self-esteem and you want to impress other people. Then again, maybe you've struggled with your business and finally made it. Your Louis Vuitton is your gift to yourself to celebrate your hard-won success. Or maybe your ex is going to be at a wedding and you want to make them jealous.

You have to drill down into the psychology of your persona.

What problem are they trying to solve? What pain can your company take away?

Continuing with our Hudson River Community Credit Union example, these are the core problems the bankers often heard from their Subpar Sams:

- *"It seems like my family is always tight for cash."*
- *"I need advice on how to handle my finances."*
- *"I need to finance my home/car/schooling."*
- *"My bad credit score is keeping me from doing what I want to do."*
- *"I want a better life for my children than I had."*
- *"I just can't seem to get ahead."*

Sam isn't looking for a financial institution with the best interest rates on CDs. He needs help getting on his feet and then trying to get ahead. The marketing message Sam wants to hear is how HRCCU can help someone struggling like him. He doesn't have enough money to worry about whether the bank across the street can offer him 0.05% better on a savings account. He doesn't have enough money for a savings account in the first place!

Mrs. Martha Mature struggles, too, but with different problems:

1. *"I'm afraid of scams or outright theft."*
2. *"I'm lonely."*
3. *"I sometimes need advice with my money."*
4. *"I don't want to be a burden to my family."*
5. *"I want to enjoy my retirement."*

Look at the second problem. "I'm lonely." How is a bank or credit union supposed to solve that? It's easy to dismiss a persona's core problems when you don't see how they apply to your company. It's not like HRCCU offers therapy. But in our Alchemyze sessions, I didn't say, "Let's not list that problem. That's not really something Hudson River can fix, right?" No, I put it on the list of Mrs. Martha's problems.

Emily the Entrepreneur has a different kind of pain:

1. *"I'm good at running my business but not so good when it comes to handling my finances."*
2. *"I often need financial advice."*
3. *"I want a relationship with my banker. I don't want to be just another number."*
4. *"I desperately want to grow my business, but I don't know how!"*

5. *"I feel the weight of making my business succeed for the sake of my family and employees."*

6. *"I wish running a business was easier."*

Just about every bank or credit union could say they already provide most of these services. While we can argue how well they do that, we can't argue that just about every financial institution offers the same kinds of products and services. Chase and Bank of America have a million Sams, Marthas, and Emilys.

Don't just offer a solution to these core problems your prospects and clients have. Create a *differentiated* solution.

———————————————————————

In the Alchemyze workbook, do "Step #4: Personas' Core Problems."

8

That Thing You Do (Already)

"To do a common thing uncommonly well brings success."

—Henry John Heinz

B y a "differentiated solution," I mean a *remarkable* solution—
something that makes your clients, customers, suppliers,
and service providers go, "You are not going to believe what this
company does! Listen: These guys are amazing. They—"

Fill in the blank. It's a story they want to tell their butcher,
baker, banker, and bartender. It's so remarkable that they can't
help but remark about it to others. It captures the imagination. It's
different from everything else out there.

At least . . . it sounds different. And, honestly, it is different.
Take a dental clinic, for example. Two dentists in the same town
might offer the same services. But are they really the same? Or is
there a difference?

Are the receptionists equally nice? Do both facilities look
amazing? Is one dentist just as helpful as the other? No, of course
not. Even if they both offer teeth cleanings and root canals, the
way they offer them is different.

Even if you offer the same thing as your competitors, the
way you do it is unique to you. Just like that office buildout

construction firm. Who else sent in a punch list guy ahead of time? No one.

You want to give your customers a story they can tell.

You Don't Know You're Remarkable

I'm often a speaker at conferences. I love doing a live Q&A where I take a person from the audience and create something remarkable from what they already do. Once, a family therapist asked how her group could market themselves differently. I asked her to quickly describe how she helped her clients' families find happiness again.

I said, "Perfect. You said there are four main phases, correct?" I drew a four-step staircase on the whiteboard. "Step one, assess. Step two, engage. Step three, intervene. Step four, sustain." I marked each of the stairsteps to match. "To me, it looks like you have a 'Stairway to Happiness: Your four-step process to move families from sad to happy.' Is that right?"

Presto. I took something she already did and gave it a name. Now, her group can market their unique approach to family therapy and reconciliation. Now, potential clients have the beginnings of a story they can tell: "You know we've been having trouble, right? Well, we found this amazing therapist, and they utilize their unique Stairway to Happiness program for families just like ours."

In another seminar, there was a woman who owned a retail store for women's clothing. She specialized in helping other women look fantastic as business professionals on a budget. Her customers had two major problems. One, they needed the best bang for their buck. They wanted to look good without spending a fortune on their clothes while *also* not buying cheap clothes that looked . . . well, cheap. Their other problem was that even when department store reps, their friends, or even personal shoppers put together amazing outfits for them, it was a specific ensemble. They looked great when they wore it, but they could only wear it so often before it started looking like they only had a few nice outfits.

Her solution was to create an *integrated* wardrobe, using a number of pieces of clothing that looked good together. That doesn't sound like rocket science, does it? You probably have a pair of slacks that look good with three or four different shirts. But this woman took it to a whole different level.

"For instance," she said from the middle of the room, "with just nine pieces of clothing, I can create thirty-six distinct outfits."

That blew my mind. I don't have thirty-six different outfits and I have way more than nine pants and shirts. In the beginning of her explanation when she talked about mixing and matching things, it didn't seem that interesting. It didn't seem remarkable. Everybody does that. But in one sentence, she completely captured my attention and made my jaw drop. I mean, look—I'm even writing about it in a book!

"What do you call that?"

She gave me the blank expression I often see.

Not wanting to embarrass her, I quickly said, "You know what I would do if I were you? I'd call it 'The 9x36 Closet: 36 unique outfits from 9 high-quality pieces of clothing.' Now, instead of trying to keep my attention for minutes on end, in just a few words you've completely captured it. It's something easy to say, easy to remember, and easy to tell others."

Name What You Do

I'm not going to belabor this idea because once you get it, you get it. Now, gather your team and start to brand or name your solutions. Each time you match a remarkable solution to a prospect's or client's problem, you have created another Remarkable. There is no limit to the amount of Remarkables you can create. And each one raises the bar for your competition to compete with you.

Let's talk about what to do when you don't sell what your client needs.

In the Alchemyze workbook, begin "Step #5: Alchemyze Your Solutions."

9

If They Need It, Make It!

"Some men see things as they are and say why. I dream things that never were and say why not?"

—George Bernard Shaw

W hat if you don't sell what they want?

What if your solutions don't perfectly match their core problems?

Here's where it gets fun.

Remarkable #1: EverStock

I once worked with an industrial chemical manufacturer that created the gloss that goes in vehicle paint. It's what makes your car, jet ski, or motorcycle shiny. The company supplied major manufacturers. GM, for one.

They typically sold through the purchasing department to provide production managers with the additives they needed. What was this persona's number one core problem? Running out of inventory. Like many industrial processes, the vehicle manufacturers ordered in bulk. When their gloss additive got low, they would order again. No matter what the customer did, though, they never could seem to time it right. But it was a major problem when they did run out because the production line would stop. That might amount to thousands or even millions of dollars in lost productivity.

"How much of your business comes from, say, your top ten customers," I asked.

"Oh, 80%, easy."

"What if you went to them and proposed something like offering to store a thirty-day supply—for free—of your product at their facility. Every month, one of your delivery folks checks how much of the extra they used. They pay only for what they use. You could call it something like 'The EverStock Program: Never run out of inventory again.' Would something like that work?"

They looked at me like I gave them the secret to life. It was wildly successful. They quickly became the number one preferred provider of their best customers, they sold extra product to their customers (without even knowing about it till the next month), and they solved the number one problem their customers faced. Of course, such a premium service earned them the right to charge a premium price. But with the cost savings from their customers avoiding production shutdowns, the customers were happy to pay a little extra. By just slightly shifting some things around in their standard operating procedure and giving the new idea a name, they were able to differentiate themselves in a literal commodity industry.

Remarkable #2: The Accelerator

Before I got into EOS, Mike and I did something like this with Square 2 Marketing several times. One of the things I'm most proud of was our Accelerator Program. One of our client's number one problems was that they needed more leads yesterday. They needed a way to significantly improve their revenues, but they wanted results as quickly as possible. As anyone who's ever run a good marketing strategy knows, good things take time. Our normal project time was six months to create the strategy, build the tactics, start the campaigns, and install the technology (we were a large HubSpot shop).

Could we do it faster? Sure, but the people assigned to that client would have to drop everything else for a month to work exclusively on one project.

"Well, why can't we do that?" I asked the team.

We tried it. I found the right client willing to commit all the necessary resources on their side to enable us to deliver an entire marketing strategy campaign in just thirty days. Oh, and who would be willing to pay the five-figure investment at the conclusion.

Our team loved it. By not having to switch between projects, they could all focus on one client at a time. They did more and better work in one month than they would have for the same project in six. The client was thrilled that their marketing was revamped and providing results in record time. Mike and I loved going from starting a contract to collecting in full within thirty days.

To roll this out to more clients, I found a firm that offered financial factoring, essentially allowing a client to pay over six months, get their deliverables in one month, and Square 2 to get paid upfront. We paid a small fee to the factoring company (which we rolled into the pricing of the Accelerator Program). We took our customer's number one core problem, solved it, and profited fantastically from it. But we had to be willing to change and consider a different and better way of doing it. The Accelerator Program was eventually responsible for just under 50% of all sales.

Remarkable #3: Emergency Copier Repair

One more example of how companies can shift slightly and prosper. I worked with a printer and copier distribution and service company. Their customer's number one complaint? The time it took to repair a printer or copier when it went down. It didn't matter that the company was better than its competitors in response time. Their typical customer was only down one to two business days. They were better than the rest. But being better than the other guys didn't solve this persona's number one problem.

The company already had thirty repair vans covering their area. While they could afford to hire another technician or two, getting them, training them, and retaining them was a serious bottleneck.

"Easy," I said. "Let's take one of your vans and call it the Rapid Response Unit. For a premium fee, anytime a customer's printer or copier goes down, you immediately dispatch the Rapid Response Unit. They're there in 59 minutes or less. Guaranteed. The right customers would gladly pay for the 'insurance' of knowing your guy is out there in one hour or less, fixing the problem and getting the team back up and running."

The marketing wrote itself. The radio ad would sound like someone making a 911 call. The caller would be a weary, worried office manager saying that their copier just died and they didn't know what to do. "Don't worry, ma'am, we're dispatching our Rapid Response Unit to your location immediately." Next thing you hear: car door slamming, seat belt clicking, and tires squealing. By the time the manager hangs up the phone, Joe is already there. "Clear!"

It wasn't a service they offered. But it was a problem they could solve with just a bit of creativity and effort. And while the other companies were scheduling service calls in a day or two, our client was making clients happy in an hour. A quick note: sometimes the <u>offer</u> of something remarkable is remarkable by itself. A large portion of new clients were attracted by the prospect of service in 59 minutes or less but ended up taking the standard service to save a few bucks. After a short period of time, our client was known as "the fast folks" and that story spread on its own!

In the Alchemyze workbook, finish or rework "Step #5: Alchemyze Your Solutions."

10

What's the Big ~~Deal~~ *Story?*

"Marketing is no longer about the stuff that you make, but about the stories you tell."

—SETH GODIN, *ALL MARKETERS ARE LIARS*

Think back to the auto parts distributor who started printing his catalog on neon pink paper. Imagine that his competitors heard about the gimmick and started printing theirs on neon paper, too. (And believe me: When you start experiencing marked success, you will inspire copycats.)

What should the guy do now?

Allow me to share something with you backed by hard science. Humans are not rational. We don't make rational decisions. Not most of the time, anyway. We make most of our decisions at a subconscious, emotional level. If that's true, then how can your marketing—something that speaks to the conscious mind—create an emotional connection with the customer's subconscious?

Stories.

If I were the auto parts guy, on the first page of my neon pink catalog, I'd tell my story. It could be something as simple as,

I started this business in 2021 in the middle of Covid while working as a mechanic. Because of the crazy supply chain

problems, my boss couldn't get the parts he needed to keep us grease monkeys busy. But I knew a guy who knew a guy. Word spread that I was the go-to person to find whatever part you needed. I just kept helping people and people kept asking for more help.

I'm still the go-to guy today. And I'm happy to hunt for what you need.

—Jim

Have you ever looked at an auto parts supply catalog, either in print or online? Nothing but products, specifications, quantities, and price. Even a story as straightforward as this one connects with people. It turns a black-and-white (and pink) catalog into a tangible object that represents a guy who knows how to hustle. A guy who likes to hunt for the parts you need. His company isn't just another part distributor. Jim humanized it. Now, there's a real person behind those pages. You're not buying from yet another company.

You're buying from Jim.

Business owners, CEOs, and marketers often get so wrapped up in selling their products and services that they forget to sell themselves. People don't want to buy from giant impersonal corporations. People want to buy from other people. They want to feel like they're part of something bigger.

Are You the Story?

Some companies' big story centers around their founder. Who can forget Dave, the founder of Wendy's who named his burger chain after his daughter? You didn't buy a square burger from a franchise. You bought what Dave promised you in his commercials.

Everybody loves the story of Airbnb. During a big conference in San Francisco, two starving artists threw a couple of air mattresses down in their living room and charged conferencegoers $80 apiece for a night's stay. Who doesn't love a cool narrative like that? How can you forget the image of a global brand starting with a cheap air mattress?

Same for Nike. Michael Jordan might be (have been?) the face of Nike, but Phil Knight was its heart and soul. Plenty of people know Knight's story from *Shoe Dog* of him selling shoes from the trunk of his car and one time having all of $5 in the business account.

People connect with these stories because they're about real people.

Is Your Customer the Story?

For Hudson River Community Credit Union, their members are the heroes of the story. Their Big Story will feature real-life people who've used HRCCU to create better lives for themselves and their families. Seniors who sleep better knowing their bank is their partner. Entrepreneurs able to grow their business thanks to their local credit union.

In their "Real Beauty" campaign, Dove did a good job of telling the stories of the women who use their products to enhance their natural beauty instead of hiding it. Uber has done something similar by telling the stories of their drivers' lives and their riders' experiences.

Maybe It's Your Mission

TOMS Shoes is famous for its "One for One" promise. For every pair of shoes you buy, TOMS gives a pair of shoes to a child in need somewhere in the world. Who wouldn't want to look at their shoes and every time be reminded about a little tyke in some developing country walking around with their own pair of shoes?

Patagonia is another great example. Its founder is an avid rock climber who wanted to pursue his sport while respecting the environment and doing business sustainably. When you buy clothes or camping gear from them, you know you're doing the right thing for the world. There's an emotional connection beyond the simple usefulness of a jacket and a tent to keep the rain off you.

Make Your Business Human

Regardless of whether your company's big story features your founder, your customers, or your mission, it humanizes you. You're no longer an idea or a faceless company. You have a face. You have a story. You give them a reason to buy from real people. You connect with them as a person.

In the Alchemyze workbook, do "Step #6: Create the 'Big Story.'"

11

Headlines That Turn Heads

"The difference between the almost right word and the right word is really a large matter—'tis the difference between the lightning-bug and the lightning."

—Mark Twain

Alchemyze is a process. You can't skip steps. You can't cut corners.

When hiring a marketing firm, the vast majority of business owners want them to come up with an awesome tagline. An amazing slogan. A phrase that blows you off your feet. Something that will make sales skyrocket so they can sell more stuff to more people.

No one ever stops to ask the question, "Are we selling to the right people in the first place?" To create a show-stopping headline, you have to figure out who you're trying to stop in the first place. That's why we don't get to headlines until step six. You have to know what you're saying and who you're speaking to.

The moment someone sees your website header, looks at your email's subject line, or reads the copy on your work trucks, they need to immediately connect with your company. All of your competitors promise the same things.

"We have the best people."

"We have the best prices."

"We've been around the longest."

"We're the experts."

If everybody says the same thing, it becomes background noise. Nobody pays attention. That's why your headline has to turn heads. To do that, your headline needs to speak to the persona's core problems.

Talk to Your Persona. Forget Everyone Else.

For the glossy paint manufacturer, it was, "Never have a down production line again." That might not mean much to other people. Your golfing buddies aren't going to say, "Wow! That's amazing!" But your persona?

They. Will. Love it.

For the people in charge of production, never running low on additives ever again would be a dream come true. For them, it's not only a headline with wow—it's a promise that sounds too good to be true.

For the office buildout firm, it was, "Love Your New Office From Day One." Plenty of entrepreneurs are uncomfortable showing that kind of emotion—especially in the male-dominated construction field. But to the office manager in charge? It's a breath of fresh air. While the competitors talk about construction expertise and budgets, this firm zeroes in on the persona's *real* problem: Making sure everyone's happy with the move.

Think back to Lion's Landscaping. The homeowner doing their online search most likely is not looking for *a* landscaping company—they're looking for *another* landscaping company. They've probably used one or several other companies in the past. They know what annoys them: they never know what's going on from one day to the next. When they land on Lion's homepage, what if the words at the top of the page read, "From Idea To Oasis In Five Steps."

They don't know what that process includes . . . but they know none of the other Baton Rouge area landscapers have a proven process. And satisfaction in just five steps? They'll think, "Wow! How did Lion's know that's what I hate most?"

(I did think about calling it their "cradle to grave" process, but someone pointed out that a graveyard is the last thing you want with your plants.)

Do you see how a headline isn't about you? **It's about your customer.**

It's Not About You

If you asked me about my two sons, I could brag on them all day long. I could talk for hours about their careers and social lives. I could show you hundreds of photos.

At first, you might be nice and let me ramble. But how long would it be before you wanted to politely exit the conversation? You don't want to hear about my kids all day long. But what about your kid? If I asked you about your kids, how long would you enjoy talking about them? Hours, right?

If your headline shines the spotlight on your company, you're doing it wrong. The customer doesn't care about you. They would never say that, but they really don't. They're looking for a solution to their own problem. They want you to shine a light on them.

With the safety products distributor, their very mission is a great headline: "Everybody goes home safe tonight." When the facility safety inspector lands on their webpage, it cuts the crap and gets right to the point: "You, Mr. or Ms. Warehouse Manager, want all your people to stay safe. Let's do that together."

You see, your headline is the tip of the spear, the start of your story. It's where your relationship with your customer begins. If your headline fails to connect, nothing else really matters in the sales process.

Headline = Movie Trailer

I once heard that Will Smith had a lightbulb moment in his career. He realized that he didn't sell movies. He sold movie trailers. It needs to be a good movie, sure, but what gets butts in seats is the trailer. If the trailer looks awesome, people want to know the rest of the story. That's what a headline is. It's the trailer to the movie. If the trailer doesn't look awesome, they won't buy a ticket to see what happens next.

Let me give you a personal example of a business's "movie trailer" that sold me on their company in just eight words. I heard a weird noise coming from the basement. I opened the door to see a foot of water covering the entire floor. Not a couple of inches. A foot.

I went to my next-door neighbor—an older guy who knows everything about everything—and told him what happened. Who should I call? He gave me the plumbers he uses.

What's the first thing I did? Whip out my cell phone and give them a call? Nope. I whipped out my phone and looked for them on Google. Decent reviews, professional website. Great pictures of their employees and their shiny vans. Do I care about their people and how clean their trucks are? No! I've got a foot of water in my basement!

I ran through a few other websites until I read a headline that stopped me in my tracks. The words at the top of their website said, "Emergency Response Time In 59 Minutes or Less." I didn't care that they were 10% higher priced than their competitors. I would have paid double!

I called, they came, they conquered. They were there in less than an hour. That company was exactly what I needed at that moment. I didn't even remember the other plumbers. The guys on my screen knew I was in trouble and needed help—quick!

One headline. Just eight words. I was glad to give them my money.

In the Alchemyze workbook, do "Step #7: Create Headlines."

12

You Don't Know What It's Like

"Customer experience is the new marketing."

—STEVE CANNON, MERCEDES-BENZ USA CEO

I once knew a woman who was hired as a marketing consultant for the sandwich maker Subway. Part of their problem was that they lost a lot of business to other fast-food places because of the customers' children. Their kids didn't like coming to Subway. They'd already rolled out a kid's menu and promoted it. What more could they do?

The beginning of her presentation was brilliant. She used a video camera (this was in the days before we had cameras on our phones), put it at the eye-level of a seven-year-old—about four feet high—and videoed the entire experience literally from a kid's point of view.

The video starts off in the parking lot. Then it showed coming in the front door. The camera panned left and right. Chairs and table legs. The camera moved to the front of the customer line. While the adult would tower above the counter to look down on the meat selections and add-ons, the kid was looking at a blank wall. The view didn't change as it moved down the line. At the soda machine, if the kid stared straight ahead, they saw boring cabinets.

From just a few minutes of video shot from a child's view, she gave the executives an idea of why kids didn't like Subway. For them, it was boring! They couldn't see what was going on. There was nothing interesting to look at. They couldn't watch the sandwich maker. They couldn't see past the plastic barriers at the pictures on the board behind the counter. No wonder kids didn't want to eat there. From what I can tell, Subway never implemented her advice, but the example stands. She let them "walk a mile in their shoes," as the saying goes.

You have to do the same.

From the Outside Looking In

As the person who runs or may have even founded your company, it's hard for you to see it from the outside looking in. For you, how you do things is "the way we do things around here." But to understand your persona, you have to see things from their point of view. What may be convenient and orderly for your company may be inconvenient and frustrating for your customer.

Let me give you two examples, both from wealth management companies.

The first is an EOS client I worked with in the Southeast. The owner is the nicest guy, but he is as rigid as they come. He could be a financial advisor in a movie, right down to the blue pin-stripe suit and plain tie. Like anybody in financial services, he had a challenge in getting new clients to sign up.

I asked him to walk me through the process of working with him. I was floored when he told me he insisted on five one-hour meetings with every prospective client to understand their needs and provide recommendations. For twenty years, he met with each prospect five separate times, in person, at his office.

I said, "Have you ever considered that's a lot of commitment on their part? I mean, five meetings? If it's a half-hour to get to your office, that's ten hours of commitment before you tell them what they should do with their money."

He said, "Well, we want to get it right."

"Yes," I said, "but your immediate goal is to close deals. And you do that by taking as much friction out of the sales process as possible. I'm picturing prospects passing on your services simply due to the commitment you are requesting upfront. I just need you to tell me what to do with my money."

He looked at me, dazed and amazed. In twenty years, it had never occurred to him even once to think about it from the client's side. Like most serious professionals, he focused on doing a great job. In his mind, that took five meetings with the prospects coming to his office.

His daughter who's about to take the reins said, "Dad, it really is too much. We need to cut this down to three meetings."

I said, "Three? Why not one?"

Now it was her turn to look at me crazy.

In the end, we shortened their sales process to two meetings. The first was cut down to just thirty minutes and would be done over Zoom. Why make people drive all the way out to your office in an industrial park if you both only need 30 minutes to figure out you're not a good fit? For the second meeting, they would make their first—and only—drive to the office to discuss what to do with their money and we expanded that to 90 minutes. In between meetings, we provided valuable additional content in the form of white papers and videos via email.

All of those extra questions and information needed from the other three-and-a-half meetings? We shifted that to after they signed up. They didn't compromise the quality of their work. We simply made it far easier for someone to say "yes" in the first place.

Wealth management example #2. The firm manages portfolios of no less than a million dollars. Yet again, they have trouble getting people to sign up. I asked what that process looked like.

"Oh, it's great!" they said.

It wasn't.

The prospects would come into the office and be seated in a waiting room. It felt very much like waiting in a doctor's office. The person assigned to your account would come get you when he was ready. You followed him to his cramped office, had a conversation about as fun as a colonoscopy, and you left. Later, they would call you up and ask if you wanted to work together.

How boring is that?

"You know what? You guys have a pretty cool office. This is, what, 10,000 square feet? You have flatscreen TVs all over the walls streaming CNBC and Bloomberg. The people in the back office are constantly moving and talking. You can feel the energy. Why don't we share that experience with your prospects?"

Today, here's what happens when you go there for the first time.

We jazzed up the waiting area and dedicated one flat screen to display a welcome followed by your name. "Welcome to Smith Capital Management, Eric Keiles!" A small but meaningful gesture to help you feel like they really want you to be there.

You would only wait a moment before one of the partners—not the one you'll be working with, but another one—would come in to greet you. He would introduce himself by saying, "Hi, I know you have an appointment with Charlie today. I'm John, one of Charlie's partners. He'll be with you in just a moment. In the meantime, could I give you a quick tour of our offices?"

You would follow him on an entire circuit around the office. More flat-screen TVs, scrolling stock tickers, people buying and selling commodities—it felt exciting, as if these people never slept. Their offices were already beautifully furnished, so no extra expense there.

Then John would end the tour by having you take a seat in their luxurious board room that they rarely used. He'd say, "Charlie will be with you in a moment. In the meantime, would you mind watching a short video that explains the history of our firm? Oh, and would you like some coffee or water, perhaps?"

John would exit and Darlene would soon enter, with a tray of coffee and bottled waters. On the screen at the head of the conference room, a three-and-a-half-minute video would play. Professionally done yet infused with the passion behind why these four partners did what they do.

Right on cue, at the end of the video, Charlie would step into the conference room. "I'm sorry for keeping you waiting. I hope they gave you a tour of the office? Great. Let's talk about why you're here today."

Then you'd have the traditional meeting of talking about finances and future goals. At the end, Charlie would say, "Eric, I believe I have all the information I need to put together a preliminary wealth management recommendation for you, but it's going to take me a few days to pull it together. But to let you know how appreciative we are of your time and the opportunity to work with you, we have donated $25 to the American Cancer Society in your name. Here's a card to show you where the donation was made."

Their close rate went through the roof. Instead of a boring meeting, we choreographed a remarkable experience. They even made sales from people who didn't sign up but told somebody else about how amazing Smith Capital was.

We didn't reinvent the wheel. We took what they had and made it remarkable.

Make It Easy

The term for this is called "experience mapping," and it's just what it sounds like. You map the persona's experience from first contact to final delivery. The more friction you can remove and the more remarkable the experience, the more they'll love the experience . . . which means they'll love working with your company.

EOS is all about process, process, process, right? Sustainable, scalable systems.

One of EOS's "key elements" is Core Processes. Each company has to document its own Core Processes. You can name them whatever you want, but they generally include these six: HR, marketing, sales, operations, accounting, and customer retention (a.k.a. customer service).

Your customer's experience should be a repeatable, scalable process, too. Of the six general Core Processes, experience mapping cuts across at least five of them:

1. Marketing: What is the persona's first impression?

2. Sales: How do they go from prospect to client?

3. Operations: What's their experience in getting your product or service?

4.   Accounting: How are they billed and what are your policies?

5.   Customer service: What happens after delivery or if there's a problem?

In the long run, HR is part of experience mapping. Even if your business is completely digital and/or automated, you still have people behind the scenes pulling the levers and turning the dials. The kind of people you hire directly impacts the persona's experience with your company.

The last step you need is a visual representation of your "proven process." An independent insurance firm we work for created the 5 D's. It's their process from taking a client from prospect to satisfied client. They made a simple step-by-step flow chart showing the five phases of the process: Discovery, Diagnostic, Design, Delivery, and Delight. When you finalize any of your processes, have your graphic designer create an image that we can showcase on your website, in the sale process, in videos, etc. It only requires a little bit of effort but will help remove the worry your prospects' might have. "These guys have figured out a process to get the results we are looking for . . . I feel safe"

So, go walk a mile in their shoes. See what it's like to be on the outside looking in. Hire secret shoppers. Ask your friends to pose as prospects. Get an outside firm to do your experience mapping. However you do it, get it done and make it remarkable.

13

"I Gah-rawn-tee!"

"A guarantee is a promise to your customers that you believe in your product."

—ANONYMOUS

Who doesn't love Louisiana cooking and cuisine?

Sure, there are plenty of celebrity chefs from the Pelican State like Emeril and Paul Prudhomme. But the original was Justin Wilson. Forget reality TV. This guy was a one-man wonder. In his Cajun accent, not only did he share the secrets to legendary Louisiana dishes but he told entertaining stories and jokes galore. His catchphrase was, "I guarantee!" But the way he said it was more like, "I gah-rawn-tee!" Almost like four words instead of two.

Plenty of business leaders don't like guarantees. They put the company on the hook. How many stories have you heard about people abusing return policies or trying to scam the store?

But done right, guarantees can be incredibly powerful.

As you know from bringing EOS into your own business, not every company needs a guarantee. I'm thinking of my client who bought adhesive chemicals from other manufacturers and then distributed them to their respective customers. Basically, they were a middleman. What could they guarantee? They couldn't guarantee shipping time because most of their product was shipped from China. They couldn't guarantee the quality because someone else manufactured it. For a commodity chemical product, those are two things that really matter. It wouldn't make sense to guarantee something trivial.

It only makes sense for
about 50% of companies to have a guarantee.

But let me share some examples and you can judge whether they're worth it.

Guarantees That Make Money

I worked with a home remodeling company once that offered their customers their 1-Nickel Guarantee. You didn't pay anything until the end of the project, and if you weren't completely satisfied, you didn't pay "one nickel."

Did they sometimes have to eat the costs from a project or two? Yes. But they made so much money from the customers who came pouring in because of the guarantee that it was well worth it.

My writing partner, Derek, offers a guarantee: "We're not done until *both* of us love your book." Here's how he explains it. If he loves my book but I don't, then he's failed in his job. If I love my book but he doesn't, then he knows it could be better (even if I don't see the problem). That assurance is wonderful. I'm guaranteed that the final product will, at minimum, meet my expectations as well as meet professional standards. No matter what happens, I'm going to get the book I want.

In fifteen years, he's had exactly one client who took advantage of that guarantee. They went eighteen months past the original timeline. Not because of Derek but due to the authors constantly changing the content and the whole concept of the book. Even then, when the project was finished, the authors gave him a 20% bonus. They felt bad for it being more involved than they'd planned and also felt like he more than earned it. Derek doesn't regret taking on the project.

Almost Guaranteed

I have a home automation client named Springboard Automation. Ever see TVs that lower down from the ceiling? Shades that automatically adjust themselves over the course of the day? Someone gives a single command to Siri that adjusts the lighting, music, and thermostat? That's the kind of cool stuff his team does.

As complicated as his equipment setups are, he didn't feel comfortable giving some kind of guarantee. He said, "But what if we gave them something like the Springboard Promise?"

"What's that?"

He said, "We promise your neighbors will *ooh* and *aah* over your home."

I thought for a second, then said, "You know? That works!"

It's not exactly legally binding. It may even be a little cheesy. But it's still better than nothing. And more importantly, it's a great sticking point when the homeowner is talking to other people about Springboard.

This may be a short chapter but guarantees deserve their own chapter because of how important they are. A good guarantee is remarkable as well as a differentiator. It also enhances the customer's experience. A guarantee removes some of the persona's doubt.

Often, a guarantee is a form of "risk reversal" where you're taking on some of the risk of the client working with you. If it's something like the 1-Nickel Guarantee, it takes almost *all* the risk out of working with you. It removes more friction.

The easier it is for them to say yes, the more likely they are to say it.

In the Alchemyze workbook, do "Step #8: Create A Guarantee."

14

How Do You Know It Works?

"Without data, you're just another person with an opinion."

—W. Edwards Deming

Y*our Marketing Sucks.*

It's a great book and makes the point that so much of what we call marketing is spending money on shiny objects and hoping it somehow magically turns into sales. "Professional" marketers talk about brand recognition, mindshare, and lots of other fluffy stuff that you can't prove. They can't trace a direct line from money spent *there* to turning into money made *here*.

For years, when Square 2 Marketing got a new client, we would send them a jar of marshmallow Fluff. We'd add a hand-written note: "We promise that this is the last fluff you'll ever get from us!" Mike and I are admittedly data nerds. What matters to us is solid data and hard facts. Because if you don't have proof, how do you know what you're doing is working?

I'll give you an example. I once worked with a consultant who ran Google Ads for several years. In sales calls, he would ask the prospective client how they'd found him.

They'd say, "Oh, I think it was on Google."

He'd press them a little further: "Do you remember if it was an ad? Or was it an organic search?"

No one could ever remember exactly. So, he didn't know if his website search engine optimization (SEO) efforts were working or whether it was the money he spent on Google Ads. Not wanting to risk it, he kept running his Google Ads.

At the beginning of one year, there was about a three-month period where his sales leads seemed to be pouring in. He said to himself, "Wow! I need to go look at the metrics from my Google Ads. Looks like I've cracked the code!"

When he logged into his Google Ads account, the first thing he saw was a red box at the top of his screen: Google couldn't charge his card on file. You see, when he lost his card around Christmas and canceled it, he forgot to go update Google. Those entire three months where his sales leads exploded? Not one of his Google ads had run. All of those prospects came from his website's SEO. (Weird coincidence, right?) He immediately canceled his Google Ad account and switched those marketing dollars over to improving his website.

You have to ask yourself the question: Are you doing the same thing? Are you spending money on one thing but getting results from something else?

In 2020, when so many people started signing up for Zoom that its servers crashed, did the marketing team pat itself on the back? "We did it! We're marketing geniuses!" No. Everybody knew the surge in demand came from the world shutting down as Covid came on the scene.

Kind of hard to miss a global pandemic. But again, this kind of thing makes you ask the question: Is something like that going on with your business? Maybe you have twice the number of inquiries this month because someone mentioned your company on a podcast you've never heard of. But since you don't know that, you might say, "Man, I'm glad we started advertising on bus benches last month. Look at our sales leads!"

Until you know, you're just guessing. Well, it's worse than that. You're assuming. And we all know what happens when you "ass|u|me" something. The only way you can really know is if you have the numbers to back up your guesses.

> *EOS is all about metrics. In chapter 5 of Traction, Gino goes over "Data," one of the 6 Key Elements. As he points out, the numbers important for each company—what he calls your Scorecard—will be different. If you have 400 different companies, you'll have 400 different Scorecards. The important thing is to figure out which ones are critical for your company. There are hundreds if not thousands of things you could measure . . . but which numbers are critical to know if things are going well or going off the rails?*

While I can't tell you exactly which metrics are important for you, I can share some of the more common ones and give examples of others. For instance, when it comes to marketing messaging effectiveness, one of the most widely used data points is your website's "bounce rate." That's the percentage of visitors to a particular website who navigate away from the site after viewing only one page, typically your website's homepage. It doesn't matter if you have a million people come to your website. If they leave immediately (or "bounce"), then you haven't accomplished anything. It'd be better if you had only a thousand people come to your website but be so interested that they stayed for a while and explored several pages. "Time on site" is another great metric to gauge whether website visitors are interested in what you have to say. The average time a person spends on a website can vary depending on the industry, device type, and target audience. Some say a good average time on a page is 50–60 seconds, while others say it's closer to 45 seconds. B2B websites tend to have the highest average time on page, around 82 seconds. Once again, your messaging is connecting with them if they are on your website for a substantial amount of time. Finally, another good metric to gauge marketing messaging is "number of pages viewed." More pages = more emotional connection with your story.

The name of the game is tracking and testing. Imagine you are tracking bounce rate and time on site. Your marketing team came up with a great new headline for your website and people started staying, on average, for four minutes at a time and the bounce rate was under 20%. *That's* how you know your marketing messaging is working.

Now, let me ask you about your close rate. Which is better? Landing one sale with every ten people you pitch? Or landing two sales with every ten people you pitch? The first one is a 10% close rate (because you sold 1 out of 10 people). The second is a 20% close rate (because you sold 2 out of every 10).

No question: 20% is twice as good as 10%.

Let's pretend your sales team closes 10% of all their sales leads. But then you implement a Remarkable like the EverStock program. The next time they make their sales presentations, they close 20% of the clients they pitch. (In reality, it was more like jumping to 50%.) That's how you know you're doing it right.

Some of my more technical clients sometimes get tripped up on making sure their data is perfect. With business metrics, accurate data is good. But what's more important is your data's changes.

Let me show you what I mean by using an example from the guy whose quote opened this chapter. In his seminars, Dr. Deming would ask, "How many people are in this room? Well, it depends on how you count them. If you're the caterer, you don't count the waiters bustling around refilling your water glasses. They're not going to eat. But if you're the fire marshal, you would count them."

Some people get hung up over whether to count the waiters or not. They get lost in the analytics. For the purposes of Alchemyzing your company, it doesn't really matter whether you count the waiters or not. What matters is that you:

1. count the same way every time (i.e., always count the waiters or never)

2. track that same number over time.

You're looking for position and direction.

I love walking parts of the Appalachian Trail. It's one of the few places on earth where I can't get some kind of signal. I have no choice but to digitally disconnect from the world and reconnect with the earth.

The downside is I have to use a paper map. Sometimes I'm not 100% sure that I am where I think I am. But I have a pretty good guess, even if I'm not GPS-accurate. Between the sun and a compass, I always know which way north is. With those two things, I can get where I'm going. From time to time, I may have to pull out my map, reorient myself, and slightly change course, but that's to be expected.

Position (even if it's not 100% perfect) and direction (even if you have to adjust your heading).

Again, I can't tell you exactly which marketing metrics make sense to track in your company. I can give you ten broad ideas that work in every company and in all the EOS implementations I've ever seen or been part of.

1. Define the Problem and Watch Key Metrics

The American engineer and inventor Charles Kettering said, "A problem well stated is a problem half solved."

Too many entrepreneurs are great at what they do but feel overwhelmed by marketing. They see it as some kind of magical voodoo. They throw money at it and hope something sticks. The truth is, you can turn marketing at any level into a process, whether it's strategic (Alchemyze it!) or tactical (How do we shorten our sales cycle?).

What problem are you tackling? What's your goal? Brand awareness? Lead generation? Website conversion? Customer retention? Referrals? You need to be clear and explicit about your short- and long-term marketing goals.

How do you know if it's working?

Key performance indicators (KPIs). That's a business-ese term that simply means, "What number tells me if it's going up or down?" While you could try to track every single thing you do, from how many mailers you send out to how many phone calls refer to a particular ad you ran, you could wind up spending your whole day looking at numbers. What you really want is one key number that tells 80% of the story.

If you've ever used Google Ads, there is a crazy degree of analytics you can dig into. But the only number that really matters is the click-through rate. If 100 people see your ad, how many take the important step of clicking on it?

If you're trying to raise customer engagement, you could look at your email engagement KPI. Out of every 100 customers on your email list, how many actually open your emails?

2. Analytics

Your KPIs give you the big picture at a glance. But as you nail down the big numbers, you can start digging a little deeper to understand how to fine-tune those KPIs.

We live in a day and age where analytics tools are cheap, fast, and easy. Take Google Analytics, for example. This incredible free tool tracks the behavior of each individual visitor to your website. You can see whether they clicked on a link from another website, found you through a Google search, or typed your web address directly. This way, you know the number one source for your website visitors. Google Analytics also tracks how long they stayed on each page, how many pages they looked at, and which links they clicked on.

While many people feel like this is Big Brother watching over their shoulder, these analytics are critical to figuring out how to run your business. The more data you can get, the more of the story you can understand.

You can take things a step further and use platforms like HubSpot, Zoho, and Salesforce to reach even deeper. These analytics can provide a deeper look into the demographics of the people clicking on your digital marketing assets. When Mike and I started rolling out HubSpot years ago, it could take some businesses a little while to get their teams up to speed. These days, it's so easy that it's almost self-explanatory.

We have the technology. We can do it better than it was. Better, stronger, faster.

3. A/B Testing

It never ceases to amaze me how many people still see marketing as black or white.

"Did the ad work or not?"

The better question is, "Did the ad work better than something else?"

When major advertising agencies roll out a new TV commercial (especially in the days before streaming), they might run one version in the Pacific Northwest and a different one in New England to see which one performed better. Once they figured that out, they would then do a nationwide commercial. Way back in the day, billboard advertisers and magazine ads would even use two different phone numbers to easily track which phone line rang more often.

That's all A/B testing is. Which version works better? Option A or option B?

The cool thing with digital marketing is that you can start getting results that same day. Whatever your website's platform, I bet it gives you the option to do A/B testing. You don't have to have two different websites. You can tweak one thing at a time.

Say you don't know which headline would turn more heads. You can go into your website's backend, enable A/B testing, and then just change the headline at the top of your homepage. Your website will automatically start alternating between the two. When Sally down the street lands on your page, she'll see version A. Two seconds later, when John from across town lands on your page, he'll see version B. Do this enough times and you'll start to see which one people respond to more.

You can do the same thing with your marketing emails, with your online ads, with your customer retention emails, with your social media posts, and just about everything else you can do online.

Of course, you can also do the same thing in the real world. You can run two different ads in two different towns. You could run the same ad in two different publications to see which one gets more responses.

Marketing isn't yes/no. It's good/better/best.

4. Easy Surveys and Feedback Forms

It seems like every website you visit these days wants you to take a survey. Every time I use an app on my iPhone, it asks me to rate it and provide feedback. As annoying as these things are, they are a goldmine for the companies behind them.

There is a whole science devoted to effective surveys, but you can get started with next to nothing. Use SurveyMonkey or Google Forms to ask your prospects and current customers for their opinion.

It would blow your mind to find out how many of your customers don't know that you sell other things besides what they bought from you. I dare you to create an email survey with one question: "Did you know we also offer [this product or service]?" The answer will bring you to tears. Companies spend thousands of dollars trying to get new people to buy their stuff. They don't know they already have a group of people happy and ready to buy more stuff . . . if they only knew you sold it.

Don't be afraid to have your customer service representatives call recent and past customers to ask them outright, "Hey! How'd we do?" Sometimes the one piece of information you need is in these quick phone calls. The customer might not take the time to write a survey response, but if they had somebody on the phone they'll often go, "Well, I was pretty happy with everything except this one thing . . . "

Don't fly blind. Ask people what they think.

5. Social Media

The same thing you do with your website or email campaigns, you want to do with your social media. Facebook, LinkedIn, TikTok, Pinterest, or whatever the latest app is almost all offer business analytics. You can track not only paid ads but everyday posts. Who clicks on which posts the most? Which kinds of posts generate the most comments and discussions? Which ones are shared more?

You can run polls and surveys. You can track the demographics of who all engages with your posts. In your own home with an iPad, you can unlock the secrets of what your prospects and customers really want.

6. Database and Conversion Rates

Let me tell you about BocaClosings, a real estate closing company that was missing out on a goldmine right under their noses. They were doing fine, but they weren't maximizing their potential. Why? Because they weren't capturing the email addresses of the realtors who come through their offices representing the homebuyers on the other side of the closing table.

Now, you might be thinking, "So what? It's just an email address." But let's do some quick math. BocaClosings was handling about 10 closings a week. That's potentially 20 new realtor contacts every week (both sides of the transaction). Multiply that by 52 weeks, and you're looking at 1,040 new contacts per year.

Here's where it gets interesting. Once you have those email addresses, you can start a drip campaign. Let's say you send out 5 emails over 3 weeks, explaining why realtors should switch to BocaClosings. In two years, that's over 2,000 Florida real estate agents in their database they can continually market to without spending a dime on advertising.

But here's the kicker: it's not just about collecting email addresses. It's about converting people into prospective clients. They need to offer them something valuable in exchange for their contact information. Maybe it's a white paper on "9 Marketing Messages to Avoid to Drive Revenue." Now they're not just collecting emails; they're qualifying leads.

In the B2B world, a good conversion rate is about 2-4%. That means for every 1,000 website visits, you should aim for 20-40 leads. These aren't just random email addresses; these are people who've raised their hand and said, "I'm interested."

The goal is to move from anonymous to exposed. Yes, your leads might feel like they're being "tortured" by follow-up emails, but that's the point. You want to stay top of mind. When a realtor needs a closing company, they want BocaClosings to be the first name they think of.

So, what's the most important metric here? It's the rate at which you're converting anonymous visitors into database contacts. For BocaClosings, it was about capturing those realtor emails at every closing. For your business, it might be something different. But the principle is the same: Get 'em in the database!

A robust, engaged email list is worth its weight in gold. It's not just about having a big number. It's about having a list of people who know you, trust you, and are primed to do business with you. That's how you know your marketing is really working.

7. What Are the Other Guys Doing?

You have to be careful with competitor analysis. Too many entrepreneurs just copy what their competitors are doing. They figure, "Hey, it must be working for them!"

What they don't know is that at the competing company, there's a marketing intern at her desk crossing her fingers and saying, "I sure hope this works!"

Don't be a copycat. Figure out what works for your company.

That said, you can glean data and insights from watching your competitors' marketing efforts. For instance, with their social media, what posts are ignored and which are hot? Do they run A/B website tests for a month and then choose one of those to run from then on?

Do some snooping around. Figure out what *is* working for them.

Then do it better.

8. Map the Customer Journey

In *Smash the Funnel*, Mike and I walk you through the "cyclonic buyer journey." Our approach to marketing completely demolishes the traditional idea of a sales funnel or sales pipeline.

The old way of thinking sees sales and marketing as a linear, step-by-step, 1-2-3 process. Human reality is not like that. It's never been. At every stage, a customer could get spun out of your universe. At any point, they may reenter it. Revenue generation isn't a nice, neat funnel—it's a series of messy, unpredictable cyclones.

You need to map your customer's experience throughout that journey. In Chapter 11, we talked about mapping the customer experience. The examples I showed are a huge part of the customer journey, but they're only one leg of the journey.

You need a map of every opportunity, every "touchpoint" your prospects, current customers, and past clients experience with your company. The more delightful and remarkable you can make each of those touchpoints for others, the better everything—from marketing dollars' ROIs to complaints to qualified referrals—will go.

Just like everything else in this book, it's a process. Map it and make it better.

And that's really this chapter in a nutshell. Figure out what you're already doing, create a scalable process from it, and then do it better, measuring the important stuff along the way to make sure you're headed in the right direction.

15

Put It into Play

"Vision without execution is hallucination."

—Thomas Edison

"**D**on't fuck it up!"

That's the phrase Chef Arya Hamedani is known for. They call him the "Don't Fuck It Up Chef."

"Yo, what's up! Today: chicken and rice. Don't fuck it up!"

"Gonna boil some noodles. Hey! Don't fuck it up!"

It'd be a shame to do all this work to Alchemyze your business and then fail at putting it into play. So—don't fuck it up!

Here's an easy eight-item list to get you started on rolling out your differentiation strategy company-wide:

1. **Burn the Boats:** Say what you mean and mean what you say.

2. **Get Everybody on the Bus:** This has to be a team effort or it doesn't work.

3. **Take It for a Test Drive:** Try out your new marketing to make sure it works.

4.   **Create Collateral ~~Damage~~ *Assets*:** Do the work to make the stuff.

5.   **Pour Gas on the Fire:** Put your money where your mouth is.

6.   **Track It:** Follow the KPIs.

7.   **1% Better:** Always find ways to constantly improve everything.

8.   **The Red Queen's Race:** Roll out a new Remarkable every 90 days.

1. Burn the Boats

You can't go off half-cocked. By nature, entrepreneurs are doers. When we have an idea, we don't sit on it. We like to take action immediately. We are the poster child for "Ready, Fire, Aim." That works well in a lot of things.

Not here.

Figure out your marketing differentiation strategy. Then commit to it. "*This* is what we're doing. *This* is our new direction. *This* is where we're headed."

I like to share the anecdote of Hernando Cortez landing on the shores of the Aztec Empire. After all his men unloaded from the boats, he set fire to them. His message was clear: There is no going back. It's either total victory or total destruction.

The story isn't true, but "Burn the boats!" has become shorthand for committing to a new way of doing things and making a clear break from the old. For your new differentiation strategy to work, you can't half-heartedly commit. You can't straddle the line with your left foot in one camp and your right foot in the other.

Do or do not. There is no try.

2. Get Everybody on the Bus

Far too often, "marketing" is a function done by those weird marketing people.

Alchemyzing your company is about changing your team's behavior. Everybody has to be on board. If they're not on board with where you're headed, they need to find another bus.

Don't expect this to happen overnight, though. It takes time to turn the *Titanic* around. You'll need multiple meetings. You'll need to continually reinforce the message. And you're not just looking for compliance. You need real buy-in.

If you're like most entrepreneurs, you constantly roll out new initiatives and new projects. This happens in corporate America every day. The people on the frontlines know that if they ignore it long enough, the new fad will go away and everything will return to normal.

That's why burning the boats is so important. Especially for you. You must believe and live out the reality that *this* is the new normal. *This* is how we do things from now on.

Lead by example.

3. Take It for a Test Drive

That said, you want to figure out how to best translate your new identity into messaging your customers respond to. I encourage my clients to try things out with key clients and select new sales prospects. Your customer service and sales teams can get immediate and raw feedback from the people you're trying to connect with.

Try some limited ads. Do a few rounds of A/B testing with your website header. As I quoted Mark Twain earlier, the difference between the right word and the almost right word is the difference between lightning and a lightning bug. Sometimes just tweaking one word can make the difference between people kinda getting it and *really* getting it.

4. Create Collateral ~~Damage~~ Assets

You have the battle plan. Now, you need to equip your people to do battle.

A list of talking points. New scripts for the customer service reps. White papers to download from the website. Images for social media posts. Videos to embed in email blasts. Infographics to pass out to prospective buyers. Landing pages. Brochures. More videos. Customer testimonials. Heck, do like Mike and me and write a book or three.

Create the tools your people need to spread the word far and wide.

5. Pour Gas on the Fire

Bill Gates once said, "The first rule of any technology used in a business is that automation applied to an efficient operation will magnify the efficiency. The second is that automation applied to an inefficient operation will magnify the inefficiency."

While doing 1–4 on this execution plan, you want to make sure you have your bases covered. You know the right words, the right messages, the right mediums, the right everything that works.

Once you have a good fire going, at that point throw some gasoline on it.

By that, I mean put your money where your mouth is. Invest (not "spend"—invest) in your differentiation strategy. Opt for the better graphic designer. Don't skimp on sales brochures. Open up the money faucet on ad spending.

6. Track It

Make sure the numbers justify the money.

We've talked about not throwing your marketing dollars down a dark hole and praying something works. Have the data to justify you're doing it right and that it's working. Let the data point you to how to do it even better.

You need to track your marketing KPIs weekly. The more quickly you can see whether the numbers are going up or down, the sooner you can respond. The quicker your response, the more quickly you'll grow.

7. 1% Better

The key concept of the excellent book *Atomic Habits* is that if you can get just 1% better every day, by the end of a year, you'll be 38 *times* better than you are today. Those little improvements add up.

Always and forever be finding ways to improve. Tweak your emails. Try a different opener with your sales scripts. No matter how good your marketing efforts, they can always be better.

Don't rest on your laurels. Don't ever feel like you've "arrived" and you can put your marketing on autopilot. Keep adjusting, keep improving, keep testing, and keep doing it week after week.

8. The Red Queen's Race

In the sequel to *Alice in Wonderland*, little Alice finds herself running alongside the Red Queen. It reads like this:

> *The most curious part of the thing was, that the trees and the other things round them never changed their places at all: however fast they went, they never seemed to pass anything.*

. . . She felt as if she would never be able to talk again, she was getting so much out of breath: and still the Queen cried "Faster! Faster!"

[. . .] And they went so fast that at last they seemed to skim through the air, hardly touching the ground with their feet, till suddenly, just as Alice was getting quite exhausted, they stopped, and she found herself sitting on the ground, breathless and giddy.

The Queen propped her up against a tree, and said kindly, "You may rest a little now."

Alice looked round her in great surprise. "Why, I do believe we've been under this tree the whole time! Everything's just as it was!"

"Of course it is," said the Queen. "What would you have it?"

"Well, in our country," said Alice, still panting a little, "you'd generally get to somewhere else—if you run very fast for a long time, as we've been doing."

"A slow sort of country!" said the Queen. "Now, here, you see, it takes all the running you can do, to keep in the same place. If you want to get somewhere else, you must run at least twice as fast as that!"

Especially in the tech world, entrepreneurs refer to The Red Queen's Race as an analogy about competition. You have to run as fast as you can just to keep up with the other guys. You have to run twice that fast to ever get ahead of them.

Of course, you can't give more than 100% effort. To really pull ahead—or to put yourself in another league altogether—you need to be rolling out new Remarkables multiple times a year. Ideally, every 90 days.

Too many of my clients (you know who you are) create three or four Remarkables. Then they stop. They rest on their laurels, believing they can keep doing the same thing and continue to scale their company. Like I said about the competitors starting to print their auto parts catalogs on neon paper too, your competitors will start copycatting your ideas when they see you having success. You can't stop rolling out new Remarkables. You have to run as fast as you can just to keep your position in the pack.

Just by Alchemyzing your company in the first place, you're going to put yourself ahead of the others. If you do it well, you'll put yourself in a whole other category completely. And if you roll out a new Remarkable every quarter, you will soon be so far ahead of the rest of the pack that they can never hope to close the gap.

Take Amazon. It's hard to imagine someone coming along and knocking them off their pedestal. Of course, we used to say the same thing about Walmart. Then again, Temu and Shein are starting to give Jeff Bezos a run for his money.

No one can (currently) touch Apple when it comes to smartphones and integrated devices. Pepsi is so far behind Coca-Cola that it's laughable. These companies did not reach a level of success and stop. They kept finding ways to raise the bar. For Amazon, e-commerce distribution. For Apple, sleek tech that works; no Windows "blue screens of death." For Coca-Cola, constantly expanding its manufacturing distribution facilities and pouring billions into branding.

You don't need to be an Amazon or an Apple. But you can be the Amazon or Apple in your market, field, or industry. Keep raising the bar. Keep being remarkable. Be remarkably remarkable.

The rest will sit around and wonder how you got so lucky.

In the Alchemyze workbook, do "Putting It into Play."

You're Wearing Ruby Slippers

Remember how at the end of *The Wizard of Oz*, Glinda the Good Witch had her big reveal? That Dorothy didn't need the good witch's magic to get back home? "You've always had the power to go back to Kansas," she told the farmgirl. All Dorothy needed to do was click the heels of the ruby slippers she'd worn ever since she arrived in Oz.

You don't need the latest CRM, the social media platform of the day, or the new sales book of the month. You don't need anything but what you already have. You simply don't know that you have the magic at your fingertips.

I promise, whatever your business, whatever your market, whatever your industry: You already do something remarkable. You can take your ordinary company and, with a little know-how and a lot of elbow grease, make it shine extraordinarily.

You are remarkable.

Let the rest of the world see that.

About the Author
ERIC KEILES

With over 30 years of entrepreneurial experience and the creation of 8 successful businesses, Eric Keiles understands the unique challenges entrepreneurs face. There were countless days of wondering, "Why am I doing this?" and moments of frustration when growth seemed impossible. Through trial, error, and relentless perseverance, Eric uncovered the secrets to breaking through those barriers.

At the digital marketing firm Square 2 Marketing he co-founded, Eric has guided over 500 companies through successful marketing transformations, overseeing more than 2,000 campaigns that turned conventional businesses into industry standouts. His approach to marketing has always centered on measurable results and practical strategies rather than theoretical frameworks. This philosophy led him to co-author *Reality Marketing Revolution* in 2007 which has sold more than 10,000 copies. He is also the co-author of *Fire Your Sales Team Today* in 2012 and *Smash The Funnel* in 2019. His insights have reached over 50,000 professionals through speaking engagements at major industry conferences and entrepreneur organizations like Vistage and the Entrepreneurs' Organization (EO).

Beyond his role at Square 2 Marketing, Eric has contributed extensively to the marketing community through more than 100 articles in publications like *MarketingProfs* and *Business 2 Community*. His innovative approaches to inbound marketing and sales enablement earned him recognition as a Top 50 Marketing Influencer by *Marketing Insider Group* in 2018.

Hitting a ceiling at $8 million in revenue was a turning point for Square 2 Marketing. Despite a talented team, loyal clients, and a suite of exceptional services, growth stalled. Searching for answers, Eric discovered EOS® (the Entrepreneurial Operating System®), a transformative methodology that provided the missing link—a system for operating the entire business. Implementing EOS not only reignited growth but also dramatically improved team morale, client retention, margins, and profits while making business ownership fun again.

Inspired by the profound impact EOS had on his company, Eric sold his share of the marketing firm to become an EOS Implementer®. Today, he dedicates his career to helping entrepreneurial companies achieve their vision and unlock their potential. Through his book *Alchemyze It!* he shares his proven six-step framework to transform marketing messaging and differentiation strategies into industry-shaping stories that drive growth, referrals, and success.

Eric lives in Delray Beach, Florida, where he remains active in the business community and continues to speak, write, consult, and mentor emerging entrepreneurs.

Other Books to Explore

Smash the Funnel: The Cyclonic Buyer Journey—A New Map for Sustainable, Repeatable, Predictable Revenue Generation

Entrepreneurs and CEOs, revolutionize your marketing with *Smash the Funnel* by Eric Keiles and Mike Lieberman. This game-changing book demolishes outdated concepts, introducing a dynamic, customer-centric model that replaces the tired funnel metaphor. Discover data-driven strategies to boost ROI, deepen customer relationships, and drive sustainable growth. Don't let competitors outpace you—*Smash the Funnel* is your essential guide to transforming marketing into a powerful revenue engine for your company.

Fire Your Sales Team Today: Then Rehire Them as Sales Guides in Your New Revenue Department

Transform your sales team and supercharge growth with *Fire Your Sales Team Today* by Eric Keiles and Mike Lieberman. This groundbreaking book isn't about elimination—it's about evolution. Learn how to reinvent your sales force as expert "Sales Guides" within a dynamic, integrated "Revenue Department." Discover a revolutionary approach that aligns sales, marketing, and service to create a seamless customer journey. For entrepreneurs ready to break free from outdated sales models, this book offers the blueprint for building a modern, customer-centric revenue machine that drives sustainable growth.

Reality Marketing Revolution: The Entrepreneur's Guide to Transforming Your Business by Building a Marketing Machine

Ready to break free from marketing chaos? *Reality Marketing Revolution* is your battle plan. Mike Lieberman and Eric Keiles reveal how to build a formidable marketing machine that delivers real results. This no-nonsense guide cuts through the hype, offering practical strategies to transform your business's approach to marketing. Learn to align your efforts with customer needs, automate your processes, and create a steady stream of qualified leads. For CEOs tired of wasting resources on ineffective tactics, this book is your roadmap to a marketing system that consistently drives growth and outperforms the competition.

Schedule a Discovery Session

U nlock your marketing potential—for free! Here's your offer for a complimentary 30-minute strategy session with one of our expert Alchemysts.

In just half an hour, gain actionable insights to transform your messaging and boost your bottom line.

No cost, no obligation—just pure marketing wisdom tailored to your business.

Don't miss this chance to revolutionize your approach!

Go to
www.AlchemyzeIt.com/discovery
now to secure your spot.

Claim your free consultation today and start your journey to marketing mastery.

Schedule a Half-Day ALCHEMYZE Workshop with Your Team!

Transform Your Marketing Message from Average To "Remarkable" To Get Results

One of the most powerful drivers of scaling a company is developing a killer marketing message. If we don't fully take advantage of who we are targeting and explain to them why they should buy from our company, then we are missing a huge opportunity to drive results. Most organizations are fabulous at what they do . . . but they stink at telling their own story. This breakdown between **inside reality** and **outside perception** is exactly what the half-day Marketing Messaging Alchemy Session was created to fix.

Additionally, another of the challenges of organizations that want to scale is <u>differentiating their companies from the competition</u>. The question "How do I make my prospects understand that we are the obvious choice to do business with?" has perplexed many business leaders and marketing and sales professionals. The Junto Consulting Team has a powerful program to accomplish this goal. They will take your leadership team through a series of deep and enlightening exercises to uncover the following:

Big Hairy Audacious Goal

You can't start a strategy conversation without agreeing where the company is headed. Popularized by Jim Collins in his groundbreaking book *Built to Last*, the first component of the marketing message makeover is developing your *BHAG*. A BHAG (pronounced "bee hag," short for "Big Hairy Audacious Goal") is a powerful way to stimulate progress. A BHAG is clear and compelling, needing little explanation; people get it right away. Think of the NASA moon mission of the 1960s. The best BHAGs require both building for the long term *and* exuding a relentless sense of urgency: What do we need to do today with monomaniacal focus and tomorrow and the next day to defy the probabilities and ultimately achieve our BHAG? Once developed, we will now have our "north star" to guide us through the Alchemyze process.

Target Market

Think about which of your current clients is your *favorite*. What would the impact be on your company if you were surrounded by the perfect clients? Building a detailed and accurate target market(s) description is the next step. We will uncover three very specific dimensions of your Target Market:

1. **Geographical** characteristics. Where are your ideal customers located?

2. What are the **demographic** characteristics of your ideal customers?

3. How do your ideal customers think and what do they value? What are their **psychographic** characteristics?

A focused buyer persona will help your team understand your ideal customer and their goals, provide guidance on how to tailor your marketing strategy, guide product development, and help you prioritize your time. When done well, buyer personas are incredibly valuable for marketing. You will also be able to use buyer personas to tailor your content so that it is relevant. This step is key to attracting the right clients but also repelling the wrong ones.

Core Problems

No purchase is ever made without solving a problem. Prospects and clients are looking for something to solve a problem, satisfy a need, maintain a desired status quo, or avert a (feared) negative experience: car maintenance, vitamin pills, anti-virus software, a washing machine. B2B purchases also fall under this category: simpler accounting software, more efficient production machinery, a more practical logistics system, etc. Understanding the most common pains and problems your prospects have when purchasing your company's products or services is an essential building block of a marketing strategy. We'll identify the most commonly heard core problems from your prospects and clients in this step.

Solutions

Can your company solve the issues uncovered and are they "remarkable"? We'll match pains and solutions and stress test the results with a brief check-in.

Alchemyze It!

If you remember, alchemy refers to the medieval forerunner of chemistry, based on the supposed transformation of matter. It was focused particularly on attempts to **convert lead to gold.** In our case, this is where the "rubber meets the road" in our session. Just because your organization has solutions for your prospects' pains, it's not enough. Those solutions must be "remarkable" to differentiate your company from all the competitive options. They are so differentiated from the competition that those offerings make prospects go *"Wow! These folks are the OBVIOUS choice to do business with!"*

We will Alchemyze the run-of-the-mill (a.k.a. boring) story of your company's offerings into something truly "remarkable." All of the differentiators we create together will comply with the two key factors: 1) unique to your organization, and 2) interesting enough that people will share your story. These will form the foundation for your overall messaging strategy.

Note: the session will deliver at least three distinct "Remarkables" that your team can begin to use immediately.

The Big Story

Forming an emotional connection with prospective and current buyers is essential to a great story. Your company's *purpose, passion, or cause* is its reason for being. Organizations that have one and live by it are more successful and endure longer than the ones that don't. We will review or identify your company's purpose, passion, or cause and connect it to the marketing message.

In this session with your team (bring as many leadership, sales, and marketing teammates as you like), you will see your company's messaging ALCHEMYZED into a story that is truly "remarkable" in your industry. In addition, leave the meeting with an action plan for your team to enhance your sales and marketing results.

The program includes:

- A 30-minute Zoom discovery call with the team to discuss your company in advance of the Marketing Messaging Alchemy Session

- Copies of our popular book, *Alchemyze It!*, for all attendees

- A complete review of your current website in advance of the Marketing Messaging Alchemy Session

- Half day virtual session (+/- three hours)

- A companion workbook for each attendee to help you start creating your own strategy during the working session

- The delivery of a summary document of the session highlighting the creation of your custom marketing messaging, specific to your business in one week or less

- A final follow-up call to discuss and finalize the messaging

Alchemyze Session Agenda

9:00 am	Introductions
9:10 am	Why Differentiate?
9:25 am	Identifying your company's *Big Hairy Audacious Goal*
9:40 am	Identification of target markets
10:10 am	Uncovering core problems for the target markets
10:30 am	BREAK
10:40 am	Matching of solutions to cure core problems

10:45 am	ALCHEMYZE IT
	(Creating your unique "Remarkables")
11:30 am	Discussion around your company's "Big Story"
11:50 am	What to expect next, Q+A
Noon	Conclude

Testimonials

"After just one day, I understand how focusing on my message, not advertising, can help me grow my business more quickly."

—TIM DAGIT, THE DAGIT GROUP

"This workshop changed the way I think about driving revenue. I'm leaning into telling my story and getting referrals more than ever"

—BARRETT ERSEK, HOLGANIX

"The best sales and marketing workshop I ever attended. My sales close rate has increased by 18% in the first quarter after the session!"

—EVERETT KATZEN, SPRINGBOARD MEDIA

Let's Connect!

Website

www.AlchemyzeIt.com

YouTube

@Alchemyze-It

LinkedIn

www.linkedin.com/company/alchemyze-it/

Facebook

www.facebook.com/groups/alchemyzeit/

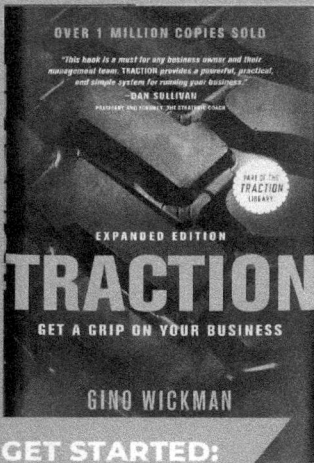

THE TRACTION LIBRARY™

GETTING EVERYONE IN YOUR COMPANY ON THE SAME PAGE

TRACTION: GET A GRIP ON YOUR BUSINESS
Strengthen the Six Key Components® of your business using simple yet powerful tools and disciplines.

FOR EVERYONE

GET STARTED:

ROCKET FUEL: THE ONE ESSENTIAL COMBINATION
Dive into how the Visionary and Integrator duo can take their company to new heights.

FOR VISIONARIES & INTEGRATORS

GET A GRIP: AN ENTREPRENEURIAL FABLE
Follow this fable's characters as they learn how to run on EOS®
and address real-world business situations.

FOR THE LEADERSHIP TEAM

WHAT THE HECK IS EOS?
Create ownership and buy-in from every employee in your organization, inspiring them to take an active role in achieving your company's vision.

FOR ALL EMPLOYEES, MANAGERS, & SUPERVISORS

HOW TO BE A GREAT BOSS!
Help bosses at all levels of your organization get the most from their people.

FOR LEADERS, MANAGERS, & SUPERVISORS

THE EOS LIFE
Learn how to create your ideal life by doing what you love, with people you love, making a huge difference, being compensated appropriately, and with time for other passions.

FOR ENTREPRENEURS & LEADERSHIP TEAMS

THE EOS MASTERY SERIES™
Dive deeper into each of the Six Key Components®
for more masterful execution.

EOSWORLDWIDE.COM